a pearl from ashes

JULIE MALLINSON

Ark House Press
PO Box 1321, Mona Vale NSW 1660
Australia
Telephone: +61 2 9007 5376
PO Box 47212, Ponsonby, Auckland
New Zealand
Telephone: +64 9 416 8400
arkhousepress.com

Ark House Press, a division of Initiate Media.

ISBN: 978-0-9875839-4-9 (pbk.)

Cataloguing in Publication Data:
Title: A Pearl from Ashes
ISBN: 978-0-9875839-4-9 (pbk.)
Subjects: Spiritual Biography
Other Authors/Contributors: Mallinson, Julie

Printed and bound by CPI Group (UK) Ltd, Croydon, CR0 4YY
Front cover illustration by Victoria Stewart
Design and layout by initiateagency.com

'Again, the kingdom of heaven is like a merchant looking for fine pearls. When he found one of great value, he went away and sold everything he had and bought it.'

—Matthew 13:45

'Who is like the LORD *our God,*
the One who sits enthroned on high,
who stoops down to look
on the heavens and the earth?
He raises the poor from the dust
and lifts the needy from the ash heap;
He seats them with princes,
with the princes of their people.'

—Psalm 113:5–8

Acknowledgements.

If I named everyone I wanted to thank, the list would be as long as the Great Wall of China .

I am grateful to so many friends and family in Australia, the United Kingdom, Canada and USA who encouraged us with prayer, Bible verses, coffee, chocolate and cereal as we lived in China. I know that it was their prayers and support that helped us get where we are today and continue to encourage us to care for orphans.

My 'foreign' friends in China always made me laugh, listened to me complain and shared my passion for the orphan,the homeless,the poor and occasionally the 'Big Mac'. The two Bevs and Natalie, Helen and Dave, Jenna,Yamid, my 'mom's group', Hollie and Rowan and Steve and Cathie... My utmost thanks to you all .

My great Chinese friends who have risked a lot to love our HIV kids as much as we do and have taught me to catch taxis with a smile - Sherry, Tina, Jo, Sarah, Jan and C Laoshi.

To all our 'Elim supporters' who gave money and time to us to help care for our Elim Kids I say a huge thank you.

A special thanks to the Elim families who have fostered, adopted and loved the Elim kids and have been willing to share their stories to help others. I look forward to an Elim kids reunion one day soon with Jenn and Jim, Rick and Cheryl, Heather and Matt and Anne and Mike.

I personally want to thank Victoria Stewart who at 16 years of age drew the amazing photo you see on the front cover whilst caring for our 3 year old Maggie.

Also, Erin Brown who patiently and encouragingly edited my

manuscript and managed to correct all my punctuation and spelling whilst still smiling.

I thank God every day for Holly McDaneld and Kathy Lee who love orphans and their Heavenly Father and obediently listened to his promptings in helping return Maggie's file to us.

I would also like to thank my lovely 12 year old, Thomas who taught me how to "cut and paste" and 10 year old James who's love for the poor and the orphans always makes me smile. As we learnt as a family 'traveling is the best education'.

My wonderful husband, Sam who has always been the calm one in the turbulent times, taught me to trust in God more every day and tirelessly supported me every time I spoke about 'the book'. He deserves extra thanks and maybe an award for patience.

Last but not least I want to thank Maggie Grace who is indeed our 'precious pearl' who wakes every day with a smile and reminds me that every child is precious to the father of the fatherless .

Contents

1. Me? A Missionary? . . . 1
2. Rice Paddies and Orphans . . . 7
3. You're Doing What? . . . 15
4. The Far Side of the Sea . . . 23
5. Viruses, Milk Scandals, and Earthquakes . . . 31
6. Tupperware Family . . . 41
7. Finding Pearl . . . 51
8. What Does the Lord Require of Us? . . . 59
9. The Least of These . . . 67
10. Living with Lazarus . . . 75
11. Help! I'm an Alien! . . . 85
12. Living with a Leper . . . 93
13. Pauper to Princess . . . 103
14. The Glad Game . . . 113
15. R2 and D2 . . . 123
16. Gum Trees and Palm Trees . . . 131
17. Too Much Turbulence . . . 143
18. Lucy . . . 151
19. Waiting . . . Worrying . . . 161
20. Happy Chinese New Year . . . 173
21. Adoption . . . 181
22. Homeward Bound . . . 189

Foreword

Amazing Grace.

Not long after we adopted Pearl, I began singing 'Amazing Grace' to her at bedtime.

We used to jokingly tell her that the song was about her. "You are amazing and your middle name is Grace," I would say.

'Amazing grace, how sweet the sound that saved a wretch like me . . . I once was lost, but now am found, was blind but now I see.'

One evening just after I turned the lights out, she spoke into the darkness. "Do you remember when God lost me?" Her little voice was filled with sadness. I tried to reassure her that God hadn't lost her, that the words to the song had a different meaning, but she was adamant.

"He did," she stated with conviction. "When I was a baby in the orphanage, but then He gave me a family and found me."

I remembered when we'd first met Pearl in the orphanage. She'd seemed so forlorn. Even though I know that God never left her, she certainly must have felt alone at those times. Abandoned. Isolated. Lost.

I considered her name, Pearl, and how we had been willing to sell everything to bring her into our family.

> *'Again, the kingdom of heaven is like a merchant looking for fine pearls. When he found one of great value, he went away and sold everything he had and bought it.'*
>
> —Matthew 13:45–46

Pearl, Lucy, Rose, and Luke have never been lost. They have always been in the hands of the heavenly Father; however, we have been blessed beyond measure to discover them in orphanages, isolation rooms and cold dirty apartments. We have been blessed as we witnessed them transform from lonely, hungry, scared children to precious children, grandchildren, cousins, and friends. God, through His amazing power, has refined them into who they are today.

> *'I will refine them like silver and test them like gold. They will call on my name and I will answer them; I will say, 'They are my people,' and they will say, 'The LORD is our God."*
>
> —Zechariah 13:9

I dedicate this book to the 147 million pearls throughout the world today. Little children who are orphaned due to sickness, war, abandonment, or poverty are as precious to Him as our Pearl is to us. I pray that these pearls will pass through the dangers, toils, and snares of life and, like our Pearl, be brought safely home to their forever families.

> 'Through many dangers, toils and snares I have already come;
> 'Tis Grace that brought me safe thus far and Grace will lead me home.'
>
> —John Newton (1725–1807)

Chapter One

Me? A Missionary?

It is hard to define the beginning of our journey to China. In our ten years of marriage we had not ever considered the prospect of moving to China. In hindsight, God had planned our future in China long before the thought had even crossed my mind.

After many years of hard study, night shifts, and work in hospitals, my husband and I were both finally general practitioners and were enjoying a comfortable life in a beautiful seaside village on the Australian east coast.

Our two boys were out of the nappy and night-waking stages, and we were experiencing the freedom of watching the kids grow up and go to school, attend birthday parties and even sleepovers without us.

We were settled and happy and talked about our 'ten year' plan, which included extensions, school fees, and a life filled with church and community activities. We occasionally talked about what we would do when the boys finished high school. Maybe we'd do some work in small towns within Australia or even go on short-term overseas medical trips.

At the time, though, we were just living day by day, trying to get ahead financially so we would have freedom in the future.

In his book *Wide Awake*, Erwin McManus described our lives perfectly: "I think a lot of us are not on a path; we're in a rut. We have confused comfort with peace, belief with faith, safety with wisdom, wealth with blessing, and existence with life. And for many of us, our dreams will be buried under the epitaph, 'I refused to let go of what I had.'"

One Sunday morning, missionaries visited our church and shared about the incredible work they were doing in Papua New Guinea. Despite their obvious passion to help the poor and needy, the mission field just didn't appeal to me. It was something that 'other people' did—a bit like becoming a triathlete or climbing a mountain. It wasn't what God had created me to do.

I was much more useful to God living and working in an affluent Australian town. And I tried to reassure myself of this as I watched photo after photo of starving villagers, medical emergencies, and dirty, sick children.

After the missionaries left, friends and I talked about them and the amazing lives they were living. It was then that I boldly commented, "I am just not one of those people who can live in another country, home school their children, and bake their own bread."

God's ways are certainly higher than ours, because eighteen months later I was doing all three! God must have been laughing nearly as much as my friend was when I uttered those words!

Missionaries were a breed of people whom I failed to identify with. They were brave and fearless adventurers who trekked for days across Africa and then cheerfully and courageously munched on pigs intestines in a bid not to offend the locals. They were knowledgeable and articulate evangelists who could quote large passages from the Bible and captivate an audience with their passion for Jesus.

They were definitely not people like me, who liked a hot shower every day, was scared of flying, and knew only the Bible verses sung on the kids' Colin Buchanan CDs.

In the Beginning

My knowledge of China was probably less than what school children know about it.

It seemed that China made every toy and trinket on our supermarket shelves. Even the fluffy koalas and kangaroos we Aussie tourists cram into every pocket of our bulging backpacks when travelling sported the MADE IN CHINA tag.

China was the home of sweet and sour pork and fried rice, and I had vaguely heard about Chinese Christians being persecuted.

Sadly, that was the pitiful extent of my knowledge.

This all began to change in January 2006.

One pleasant evening while at a barbecue and pool party, As the sun set and the boys careened down the driveway on their tricycles, a friend and I sat and sipped tea, putting off the inevitable fact that soon I would have to load a protesting six- and three-year-old into the car and drive them home for the dreaded bath-and-bed routine.

We were on our second cup—or was it pot?—of tea when we arrived at the age old question: would we have any more children?

I was quick to answer with an emphatic no! Despite the frequent enquiries as to whether I would 'try for a girl', I was unwilling to risk another nine months of almost constant nausea for a 50 percent chance of having a little princess. I was destined to remain a soccer, car, and train Mum, not a ballet, hair-clip, and fairy one! I joked about this to my friend Judy. "The only way I would have any more children is if I were guaranteed a girl and I could avoid labor and pregnancy."

She told me about friends who had recently adopted a girl from China and how well she had settled into their family.

We spoke briefly about adoption, China, and the needs of orphans worldwide. Of course I had heard about orphanages in China and had dim memories of phrases like 'one-child policy' and the oversupply of girls due to the cultural need for boys. But the situation was a distant thought in my busy life.

We finished our tea and I reluctantly bundled the two tired boys into the car.

That night I couldn't rest without thinking about the Chinese children my friend spoke of. Were orphanages there really filled with Chinese girls? Did they go to sleep every night feeling lonely and unloved? Were any families adopting them, or would they remain in orphanages?

Throughout the following week, thoughts of these children and the possibility of adoption haunted me. I wasn't imagining a cute little girl playing in our house, but rooms full of unwanted and unloved girls in a country that was only an eight hour flight away.

I spoke to my husband, Sam, about my feelings. Instead of the shock I expected, he reacted calmly and promised to pray for guidance as to whether the adoption pathway was for us.

I waited impatiently for God's guidance and a sign to show me the plans He had. I secretly hoped for a text message, screen saver, or note on the pillow saying, "Julie, please adopt an orphan from China. Signed, God." It would take something pretty obvious to convince me that this was the path He had chosen for our family.

Instead, God chose to speak to me through people, His Spirit, and His Word.

Soon after that first conversation, I received a prayer request brochure from an overseas mission organisation. There in bold across the front was a verse that I had never seen before—despite having recently read the 'Bible in a Year': '*God sets the lonely in families*' - Psalm 68:6.

Talk about a letter from God! It had never before crossed my mind that He had a plan for the lonely, and I started wondering if adoption was one of the ways He showed His love to those without a family. That God could actually set a lonely child in our family amazed me.

Days later, during a phone conversation, I explained my predicament to a Christian friend; then I hesitantly asked her opinion. "Do you think that is what God wants us to do?"

I expected her to deliberate, discuss the effects of removing a child from her culture, the changes it would create in our family, and maybe even offer prayer. Her response stunned me. "That's a great idea! Why wouldn't God want you to do it?"

She encouraged me to follow my heart and do a Google search on adoption and Chinese orphans. We spoke about the importance of listening to the whispers from God and I hurriedly hung up so I could begin my search. I was so excited I almost forgot to eat lunch!

As I sat at the computer screen, I was transfixed by the photos and stories of these unwanted children. Some were pale and malnourished and some looked healthy with rosy Chinese cheeks. But all had emptiness and sadness in their eyes.

I stared at these kids and couldn't help noticing the stark differences in our surroundings. These orphaned children, with their sad little faces, had nothing. They sat in rooms, void of any toys. Our computer was in the boys' toy room. I glanced around at the multiple trains, cars, books, and more that surrounded me. The gross inequality troubled me.

As I looked at those faces, I felt as if I had just received a lot more than a note from God to adopt! He had sent me pictures, too! As they say, a picture speaks a thousand words.

Over the next few days and weeks, Sam and I increasingly talked about the possibility of adoption, and we continued to feel that God was answering us with a resounding yes!

We went to Tasmania to celebrate our tenth wedding anniversary and spent many hours discussing, reading, and praying as we sat by the open fire in our log cabin. Finally we made the first phone call from a public phone booth in Northern Tasmania. Even though it was a cold, rainy February day, we both had such peace in our hearts as we rang the Department of Community Services (DOCS) and ordered our adoption information pack.

The next few months were a blur of seminars, paperwork, interviews, and even more paperwork. I eagerly read every book about adoption that I could find at the local library. We even tried to embrace some of the Chinese culture. The boys were happy with sweet and sour pork and fried rice, but warm soy milk for breakfast was not such a hit!

Throughout the process we were honest with the boys and told family members and some friends about our plans. All were very supportive and interested, which was great. Thomas had just started kindergarten and James had recently turned three. Both embraced the idea of a sister from China, and at one point James proudly told a friend that he wasn't going to get a puppy; rather, he was going to get a sister from China!

A few weeks after the beginning of the school year, the school had an open day so that parents could observe the classroom, meet the teacher, and so on. I was an eager kindergarten Mum and went along with a friend. We admired the sight words posted on a bulletin board, perused the school books, and noted the reading corner. Then we turned our focus on the artwork adorning the walls. All the children had drawn pictures of their families.

As many parents know, six-year-olds' drawings look pretty much the same. I scoured the walls for Thomas's drawing. Finally I spotted it hanging in the centre. In Thomas's masterpiece I was in the middle, looking remarkably tall and thin—unrealistically, I hasten to add—surrounded by Sam, Thomas, and James. To the side was a small brown four-legged creature labeled 'Grace', the name we had chosen for our Chinese girl.

"I didn't know you had a dog," my friend commented.

It was news to me too.

The next morning I asked Thomas about it. Without looking up from his breakfast, he said, "It's the girl from China, Mum." His voice revealed frustration at my lack of knowledge.

"But, darling, you know we won't be getting her for years."

"I know, Mum, but I didn't want her to feel left out when she did come. I want her to know that we were thinking about her."

Tears welled in my eyes (and still do) at the compassion and love my six-year-old boy demonstrated. It amazed me that he could think ahead to protect the feelings of someone he had never met.

A year after we had called DOCS, our file was logged in with the centre of adoption affairs in Beijing.

Our long wait for a Chinese girl had just begun!

> *'For my thoughts are not your thoughts, neither are your ways my ways', declares the* LORD. *'As the heavens are higher than the earth, so are my ways higher than your ways and my thoughts than your thoughts.'*
>
> —Isaiah 55:8–9

Chapter Two

Rice Paddies and Orphans

Sam and I continued our interest in adoption and China. We became members of a number of support groups for people adopting internationally and enjoyed reading the emails from other waiting parents, visiting adoption websites, and seeing the joy in families when they were finally matched with a much-wanted child.

One day Sam called me to come and watch something on the computer. Usually this was a good soccer goal or an equally unexciting news item, so I didn't hurry. This time, however, he showed me an amazing video reconstruction of a Chinese mother abandoning her infant daughter with great sadness and heartache. The video then continued to show many dejected faces of children in orphanages.

We watched the video over and over, wondering how a Mum would feel giving up her own baby, and how those lonely children would feel without the love of a family. The video was promoting an American organisation called 'Bring Me Hope,' which ran summer orphan camps.

We could easily manage this and it was definitely something that would fit in nicely with our lives. It sounded like a fantastic opportunity to serve and love these precious children, while at the same time incorporating a China holiday. I wouldn't have to home school the boys or bake bread, and our comfortable house would be waiting for us on return. Perfect!

So in the middle of July, the heart of Australian winter, we packed our bags, lice shampoo, and craft supplies and headed to the Northern Hemisphere.

Prior to attending camp, we travelled throughout China for two weeks. We sailed down the beautiful Li River surrounded by limestone cliffs and mountains, tried our hand at bargaining at the riverside markets, and battled the crowds of Chinese tourists at the Great Wall and Forbidden City.

In many ways China was similar to what we had expected: hot, crowded, and very busy. Wherever we went we were pressed in by masses of Chinese people, and we began to realize the implications of living in the country with the highest population in the world.

We had some wonderful Chinese meals of Beijing duck, bamboo cooked rice, and beer-battered fish. We were also very happy to have more familiar meals at McDonald's, KFC, and Pizza Hut!

Immediately prior to attending the 'Bring Me Hope' camp, we ventured up the mountains to visit the world heritage rice paddies at Long Shen. We travelled three hours from Guilin. Along with ten other tourists, we were cramped in a minibus. Poor James managed to vomit the entire contents of his breakfast within ten minutes of departing. After that it was a quiet journey as our crowded and now smelly bus wound its way up the mountains.

Once we arrived at the foot of the mountain we still had a forty-minute trek up the hill to the tiny village nestled on the hillside where we would be staying. Sam and I lugged our suitcases up the steep incline. Much to the amusement of the locals, the boys were treated to the luxury of being carried in a sedan chair!

We thoroughly enjoyed being high in the mountains with so few people around us. Already the boys had grown tired of the attention of many well-wishing locals. Sam and I were more than happy with a break from the seemingly life-threatening task of crossing the road in a Chinese city.

We sat on our balcony and admired the hundreds of rice paddies. We watched the midsummer sun shimmering off the paddies and the occasional farmer bent over his hoe as he cultivated the dirt in the searing heat.

The boys and I managed to venture even farther up the hill one morning and watched the sun rise over the mountains with the clouds low in the valley. We were awestruck at the beauty of creation and especially that we stood higher than the clouds!

Being foreign tourists, we hadn't realized that tiny mountain-top villages don't accept Visa cards. Our $5 had to last us four days. We survived on a diet of rice crackers and water. Despite the lack of good food, having to cope with squat toilets, and poor James suffering from diarrhea, all went well and we enjoyed a well-earned rest after the hustle and bustle of the overcrowded big city.

However, on our last night I was unable to sleep due to a combination of the heat, a buzzing mosquito, and a hard Chinese bed. My mind started working overtime as the boys and Sam slept soundly, oblivious to my tossing and turning. What if someone gets appendicitis? How would we get down that hill and to hospital? Which hospital would we go to? Because of the language barrier, how could we describe to the doctors the symptoms? Are there doctors in China? Do they even know what appendicitis is in China? Worse than the annoying mosquitos, these thoughts circulated in my mind, a never ending cycle of worries.

Finally I got out of bed, picked up my Bible, and sat in the relatively cool breeze on the balcony. I glanced out over the rice paddies and occasionally saw a light shining from a distant farm house. I opened my Bible to a verse that comforted and strengthened me.

> *'If I go up to the heavens, You are there; if I make my bed in the depths, You are there. If I rise on the wings of the dawn, if I settle on the far side of the sea, even there Your hand will guide me, Your right hand will hold me fast.'*
>
> —Psalm 139:8–9

Immediately I felt God's peace fill me as I realized that not only was I on the other side of the sea, but I was high up in the 'heavens', surrounded by rice paddies and clouds, yet He promised that He was with me.

I eventually returned to my hard bed and, despite the heat and buzzing mosquito, drifted into a contented sleep.

Like Paul in the Bible, I have asked three (or is it three thousand?) times for God to change me and make me less anxious. So many times I have wondered why I just don't look at the rice paddies in life instead of the appendicitis attacks.

One day I read a brilliant sentence written by Elizabeth Elliot in her book Secure in the Everlasting Arms: "We are meddling with God's business when we let all manner of imaginings loose, predicting disaster, contemplating possibilities, instead of following, one day at a time, God's plain and simple pathway."

How often I can be accused of meddling with God's business! I am thankful that during that night in Long Shen, He gave me comfort and a verse that could guide me, comfort me, and encourage me over the ensuing years.

Needless to say, no one got appendicitis. And as the sun rose and once again reflected off the never ending rice paddies, I realized how crazy I had been to worry. Amy Carmichael said that it is in the middle of the night that all of life's molehills become mountains. I know too well that I am not the only one who has experienced the wisdom in her words.

We journeyed back to Guilin and were happy to visit those famous golden arches. We took with us memories of the world heritage rice paddies. My best remembrance is of how God had assured me that He is always with me.

'God has said, 'Never will I leave you; never will I forsake you."

—Hebrews 13:5

Bring Me Hope

We spent the last week of our China holiday as volunteers at the 'Bring Me Hope' summer camp near Beijing. Volunteers were paired up with a Chinese university student and an orphan. The university student would act as a bridge between the child and the volunteer. He or she would translate and help with cultural issues. Families and orphans did crafts, braved the swimming pool, and formed a special bond that would remain with them forever.

Despite repeatedly being encouraged to come to camp with no expectations, I couldn't help but have one or two. First, I came with my bag packed full with beads and bracelets and tiny soft stuffed koala toys. Second, I secretly expected to be matched with a five-year-old girl, preferably with pigtails.

Instead I was matched with three teenage girls—one who was bigger than me! I tried my hardest to bond with these girls despite the heat, lack of a common language, and their lack of interest in my toy koala collection! At times they were more like annoying little sisters than the cute daughter I had hoped for.

When we took the girls to the Great Wall, I nearly went grey in a day. My translator was eagerly taking millions of photos, whilst the eldest girl (the one bigger than me) was more interested in making sure her hair was done than in climbing the wall. My youngest girl continuously ran ahead despite the over 40 degree heat.

I returned to camp tired, hot, and frazzled after a day trying to coax one girl to walk slightly faster and ensure the other didn't run across China!

One night the mosquitos seemed to go on a feeding rampage, biting everyone. The next morning many of the children were covered with infected and bleeding sores, which were driving them mad with the constant itch. As Sam and I were the resident doctors, we were kept busy applying antibiotic and anti-itch creams and cold compresses. Two children didn't suffer from the attack of the mosquitoes: Thomas and James. Over their protests, they had been liberally sprayed with insect repellant by their doting parents.

Although my girls didn't need me as much as I had hoped or expected, I had seen situations that exemplified the hardship of life as an orphan. One day whilst Sam helped Thomas and James take off their swimming clothes and wring them out, I noted his six-year–old 'buddy' quietly folding his own clothes and placing them in a neat pile. He had never had a Dad to help him with simple tasks like that.

On the last night we experienced a huge storm complete with thunder and lightning. It felt so near that I expected that our dorms would be hit by lightning at any moment. As the thunder grew louder and the lightening brighter Thomas and James both scurried into my bed for reassurance. We lay in bed under the mosquito net, huddled together for protection. I tried not to imagine all the other kids who had no parents to cuddle up to. I couldn't help thinking that being an orphan meant no one to run to in a storm, no one to prevent mosquito bites, and no one to help with the everyday tasks like folding your clothes. Being an orphan meant isolation, loneliness, self-sufficiency, and heartache.

The last day of camp dawned bright and sunny although the mood was not. Even I was saddened to think we were about to return the children to the only 'home' they knew: an orphanage.

One of our last activities was for the camp to gather together and read the good-bye letters we had written to each other, each one listening to the good-byes from the other 'families.' I despondently listened to the words being read. Words written by sad and tearful children who had experienced love for the first time. Words written by Chinese university students who had formed friendships that would soon be severed. Words written by Americans and Australians who had grown to love a child in just five days and couldn't bear the thought of seeing them return to an unknown future. As the letters were read, the child, volunteer, and translator were all in tears as the close bond they had formed would soon abruptly end.

Probably forever

Then it was my turn.

What my oldest girl wrote shocked me. The few words she wrote would haunt me in the middle of the night for many months: "Thank you for coming to China to play games and do craft with me. I had a lot of fun. No one has ever been as nice to me as you have."

My initial guilt at not being nicer quickly turned to surprise. I, the disgruntled, hot, spoiled foreigner who had been impatient with this teenager when she lost her water bottle and was annoyed when she refused to go swimming, was the nicest person she'd ever met? What on earth had happened to her? How had people treated her?

That statement affected me more than any photo of a baby in a cot or any story about 'dying rooms.' Here was a girl who had never ever been treated nicely in the sixteen years of her life! "To the loved, a word of affection is a morsel; but to the love-starved, a word of affection can be a feast." These wise words of Max Lucado rang true. To her the seemingly small amount of love and patience I had shown had seemed like a feast.

Those few words made it even harder to bear the good-byes. My three girls quietly returned to their room, packed their few belongings and a toy koala each, and headed out to the minibus that would take them 'home.'

All of us were emotionally drained as we watched a bus full of wailing children pull away to take the children back to the orphanage. Many tried to hold their volunteers' hands through the windows as the bus drove off. Maybe it would be their last gentle touch for a very long time.

After they left and we dried our tears, the staff and volunteers sat around and debriefed for a few hours, with the help of some much-needed Starbucks coffee. I was relieved to hear that others were feeling as emotional as I was. But I was shocked and saddened to hear the stories they had to share. Two little boys who were from a poor foster home had never seen running water before. The excitement of seemingly unlimited food supply, many foreigners, and running water made one of these boys ask, "Are we in America?"

One volunteer shared about the difficulties she had with her little boy. He seemed not to want to be with her group at all and was repeatedly running off to join another 'family' group. On the last night she had listened to him as he shared his life story—the high and low points of his short life. The low point had been a few years prior when his parents had been killed in a fireworks accident. He and his brother had been separated and sent to different orphanages. His high point? Seeing his brother again two years later!

"When did you see your brother again?" the volunteer gently enquired with the help of the translator.

"This week," answered the boy, incredulous at the foreigner's ignorance. "That's him over there."

And there he indeed was, the family group he had been running away to was actually his biological brother, whom he hadn't seen for two years!

We laughed later that it would have been nice to know such information sooner. But at the time we were all devastated for this little boy who had become an orphan overnight and concurrently had to cope with the grief of losing his parents and being separated from his brother.

After we debriefed we packed our bags and prepared for the journey home. Camp was over. School, preschool, and work awaited us in

Australia. So it was with heavy hearts and heavy bags full of chopsticks, silk scarves, and I CLIMBED THE GREAT WALL T-shirts that our family boarded a plane in Beijing headed for Sydney, Australia.

"The next time we are in China, we will be coming to pick up our baby," Sam and I joked as the boys fell asleep with their heads on our shoulders.

Would that even be possible?

> *'I know, O LORD, that a man's life is not his own; it is not for man to direct his steps.'*
>
> —Jeremiah 10:23

Chapter Three

You're Doing What?

After returning to Australia, Sam and I both felt unsettled, and also that our help to the underprivileged in China was to have a wider scope. We found it hard to feel comfortable back in our community and felt less concerned about the things that had previously occupied our thoughts, time, and energy. Just getting by in the busy Western world seemed to be taken up with work, trips to school, homework, and attempting to keep the house in order. Our hearts just weren't in it anymore. Life in the 'lucky country' had lost its luster.

Sam would later describe it as a 'holy discontent.'

Over the past six months, I had been fervently praying that God would remove my heart of stone and replace it with a heart of flesh - Ezekiel 36:26. Unfortunately, I discovered the hard way that the heart of 'flesh' caused sleepless nights and resulted in my being very uncomfortable in my more than comfortable lifestyle.

How often I had stood in church and absently sang lyrics such as 'Break my heart for what breaks yours', but never expecting to end up with a broken heart. My heart was well and truly broken now for the plight of the orphans as my thoughts would return to my Chinese girls and Sam's would return to his Chinese boys, whom he had bonded with. He worried that they were on the brink of depression.

We began to talk about when we go back to China rather than if! We were both convinced that if we could find a way to utilize our medical skills to serve in China, we wouldn't hesitate to go. Our passion and calling was to help care for Chinese orphans, we just didn't know where to start!

I began to spend hours on the Internet, looking for an organisation that would welcome two lowly general practitioners with two young children. After a few weeks of searching, we found a company that seemed to be a great fit. It was looking for doctors to work in the orphanages, and, in particular, it wanted a female doctor not only to provide medical care to the many workers in the orphanage but also someone to train village doctors, who often had little or no education.

This was perfect for our family and skills. I had spent many hours in women's health and Sam loved teaching. It seemed like the job opportunities had been planned for us ahead of time. I confidently believed that the One who went before Moses in a pillar of cloud and fire was also going before us and preparing the way.

We would go to China for one year and then return to resume the wait for our healthy baby girl, Grace, whom we hoped to be allocated to us in the next few years.

Looking back, it is astounding to think that I did a Google search for 'Chinese orphans, medical volunteer' and then six months later stood in an orphanage in Central China. Such is the power of God that He can use the Internet and someone as computer illiterate as me and still be able to guide the way!

We were excited and nervous at the same time.

Again and again it was confirmed that this was the path that God had planned for us and, although at times daunting, that this was the next step in our lives.

We managed to find a new doctor to take over Sam's position in the practice, rent out our house and even our cars, and pack up our belongings. I even got my head around the thought of home schooling our boys, which initially had terrified me.

Every now and then I would be suddenly overcome with fear and the absurdity of what we were doing. What normal people would pack up everything and move to China? The doubts would always surface when well-meaning friends and family asked us many questions.

"You are going to home school? I could never do that."

"How many foreigners are in the city where you'll be living?"

"What will your house be like?"

"Do you have to take your own towels and pots and pans?"

"Do you speak Mandarin?"

"Do you know anyone in China?"

As I answered these questions, or tried to, the reality began to weigh on me. We were moving to a country where we knew no one, didn't speak the language, and would be forced into a drastic lifestyle change. Known for losing my patience during the ten minutes of daily spelling homework, I would be home schooling two boys in a house that may or may not have pots and pans. Sometimes I would just feel plain overwhelmed at the prospect of what lay ahead of us.

One day when particularly engulfed by all the unknowns, I retreated to my bedroom to read the Bible. As I sat on my bed, peering through the kookaburras and gum trees, I spotted the beautiful Pacific Ocean. I contemplated that in a few months' time, my bedroom view would be far different.

I picked up my Bible and opened to the book of Exodus where God told Moses to leave Egypt and go to the Promised Land. One verse particularly encouraged me.

'My Presence will go with you and I will give you rest.'

—Exodus 33:14

God's peace calmed me. Though I would be home schooling, living in a foreign country, not knowing the language or understanding the customs, and eating strange food, He assured me that His presence would be with me and would give me rest.

The day arrived in March 2008 that our bags were packed. We said good-bye to family and friends and left sunny, blue-skied Port Stephens for central China.

As the plane flew over the barren Australian desert the boys and Sam settled into the on- flight entertainment. I thought about all that we were leaving and the unknown we were entering and reminded myself that soon I would be 'settling on the far side of the sea' and He would be with me.

'Have I not commanded you? Be strong and courageous. Do not be terrified; do not be discouraged, for the LORD your God will be with you wherever you go.'

—Joshua 1:9

Before getting settled into our new home in China, we spent two days touring Hong Kong while on our way to visit friends working in a remote village in Nepal. We survived the hustle and bustle of Kathmandu airport and emerged intact, to be greeted by the smiling face of our friend Ana.

It was refreshing to see a familiar face after feeling very much like foreigners on the crowded flight packed with Nepalese and Chinese, all chattering away in foreign languages and filling the overhead luggage compartment with all sorts of strange objects like buckets, cartons of eggs, and what looked like dehydrated fish!

A few days prior to leaving Australia, we learnt that this was not the best time to travel to Nepal. It certainly wasn't the worst, but we were arriving two days before the momentous 2008 election, and there was a lot of political turmoil and unrest. I tried not to listen to the news reports prior to our departure and trusted our friends who reassured us that, although the country was in turmoil and there were shootings and bombings, we foreigners in a tiny village in the mountains would be well out of harm's way.

After a twelve hour minibus ride, we arrived in the little village where our friends Ana and Steve were working. Thomas and James were amazed and thrilled to see such a tiny town with no roads. They enjoyed running around the well-trodden paths, followed by the occasional goat. They loved playing with the local children, exploring the big garden, and climbing mountains.

Sam and I were intrigued and humbled to see the Nepali houses, which looked more like old tin sheds with tin roofs weighed down by pebbles. I saw for the first time women waiting in line to collect their daily water supply from the common well that supplied the whole town.

Nepal was well into 'load shedding', meaning that for at least six and maybe even more hours a day the electricity was shut off. This worked on a roster system, and we would busily try to fit showers, cups of coffee, cooking, and watching TV into those hours when we were fortunate enough to have electricity.

Two weeks later on our arrival to China, I was surprised when James asked, "What hours do we have electricity today?" I marveled at how a quick trip to Nepal changed his taking things like electricity for granted.

We enjoyed visiting with our friends and meeting their foreign friends, many who worked as doctors, nurses, and physiotherapists in the mission hospital there. It was encouraging to see such a lovely bunch of 'normal' Americans, Australians, Swiss, and Canadians living in the middle of nowhere, serving God and the people of Nepal with love and compassion.

When we informed them that we were on our way to China, they looked at us with shocked expressions. They commented on how brave we were in choosing China, a country known for its persecution of Christians. I was reminded of twenty years prior, when embarking on the six years of study to become a doctor, that other university students would falsely assume that I was brave.

I didn't feel brave then, and I didn't at all feel brave now. To tell the truth, it did unnerve me a bit that people living in a tiny village in Nepal in the middle of civil unrest would think that I was the brave one. I secretly hoped they didn't know much about China!

As Nepal's Election Day approached, a continual drum beating surrounding our village increased. The competing parties constantly marched around the village, chanting and banging drums. We huddled around our friends' tiny transistor radio and listened to BBC news to hear about the recent bombs and killings. Most were in the capital, Kathmandu, but the violence was increasing in a number in the villages.

One day, our friends were travelling with us to a neighbouring village via minibus. Our bus was stopped as it bumped over the treacherous road by Maoist troops, many who were only young teenagers and had been forced into the army. My calm demeanor flew out the window and fear went into overdrive. I pleaded with God for safety and specifically the safety of the boys, who sat innocently in the backseat playing with their new Transformer toys. "Please keep the boys safe. They haven't done anything wrong. They are innocent. They didn't even plan this trip to Nepal."

After a five-minute chat with the bus driver and nervous glances at the foreigners in the backseat, the troops went on their way. The boys were safe, Sam courageously took a few photos, and my heart rate slowly returned to normal as we drove away.

The next morning, whilst sipping coffee made with milk powder and overlooking the valley immersed in fog, it occurred to me how hard it must have been for God to see his Son suffer. Jesus, far more innocent than my sons, was falsely accused, tortured, and killed. How hard for a parent to witness a child who was needlessly suffering. How hard just to stand by and watch.

> *'He was oppressed and afflicted, yet He did not open His mouth; He was led like a lamb to the slaughter, and as a sheep before her shearers is silent, so He did not open his mouth.'*
>
> —Isaiah 53:7

It was at that moment, far away from home, with Easter services, communion, and Bible study groups that I fully realised the great sacrifice He made for our sins.

> *'He was despised and rejected by men, a man of sorrows, and familiar with suffering. Like one from whom men hide their faces He was despised, and we esteemed him not.'*
>
> —Isaiah 53:3

After two wonderful, eye-opening weeks in the village in the mountains of Nepal, we once again braved the twelve-hour bus trip to Kathmandu to prepare for our flight to China.

Kathmandu teemed with traffic, dust, and piles of rubbish taller than I was. Malnourished dogs ran wild around the streets. Our taxi was often surrounded by dirty, homeless, barefooted children who banged on the windows, hoping for some spare change.

It was hard to believe that only three weeks prior we had been living on the pristine east coast of Australia. Even more difficult to accept was that in twenty-four hours, we would be in a different city. One we would call home for the following twelve months.

That last night in Kathmandu, we stayed in a guest flat owned by a Christian Nepali couple. Though it was probably two stars by Australian standards, it was luxurious for Nepal. And after a grueling twelve-hour bus ride, even the cold shower didn't worry me.

Whilst waiting for our taxi to the airport the next morning, we stood in the small lounge room as the sun streamed in through the dust-smeared window. The boys happily played with their cars, Sam read the newspaper, and I scanned the many inspiring titles crammed on the bookshelf. I picked up a book by Noel Piper, Faithful Women and Their Extraordinary God. A quote on the first page jumped out at me: "Missionaries are ordinary people who believe in an extraordinary God." The book was filled with inspirational stories about missionaries all over the world. None of them seemed to be ordinary people, but it quickly became clear that they all had started off just like I was—an ordinary person believing in an extraordinary God.

Surrounded by the sights and smells of Kathmandu, I realised that I could, indeed, be classified as a missionary, which would be confirmed again and again throughout my time in China.

Although I am sure there are trans-Africa-trekking, pig intestine–munching 'missos', many people just like me, normal by anyone's standard, serve on the mission field throughout the world. We battle doubts and fears, and at times our faith is challenged. We experience sleepless nights, worrying about the safety of our children, and some days the craving for a cappuccino is enough to send us 'home' on the next plane out.

The one thing we all have in common is an extraordinary God—a God whose love is unfailing and who daily forgives us our sins; a God who is powerful; a God who sees the lonely and broken-hearted and brings comfort to them; a God who sees the sick and brings them healing and hope.

I boarded the flight to China with a peace that I had never experienced before. And frankly, it defied all human reasoning. But that's the nature of being in God's will. Though uncertainty is on every side, God's presence quenches fear.

So only hours before arriving in China God showed me that I was, indeed, a missionary.

> *'For I know the plans I have for you,' declares the* LORD, *'plans to prosper you and not to harm you, plans to give you hope and a future.'*
>
> —Jeremiah 29:11

Chapter Four

The Far Side of the Sea

Our flight from Kathmandu to Xian was long but uneventful. Despite our exhaustion and that the food we were served on the flight was unrecognizable, our excitement increased as we approached our destination—a city of nine million people and where we would live for the next year.

What will our house be like? What will the other foreigners be like? Will we survive? Will we have friends? Countless other questions hurtled through our tired brains.

Sam prepared his video camera to record the plane descending into Xian. We were flying through clouds, but we craned our necks to catch our first glimpse of Xian. Twenty minutes later, our plane was still shrouded by thick, grey 'clouds' when we heard and felt a loud bump as the wheels hit the tarmac.

We had landed!

No city lights to see or ancient Chinese buildings. Just a thick blanket of pollution that covered the ground.

Now we knowingly laugh at how naive we were to attempt to video our first landing.

Our first few weeks in China were a blur of 'squishy' buses, fantastic Chinese food, and getting to know our incredible Chinese staff and the other foreigners in the city.

We explored the city with the boys, walking on the famous wall, visiting historical sites, and sampling many plates of noodles, eggs, chicken, and sweet and sour pork. Not all of our food experiences were welcome ones. The boys still remember our first pizza topped with tomato paste, banana, apple, cherries, and liberally covered with cheese!

We also slowly learnt to navigate the challenging aspects of living in a new city and country.

Attending our medicals so that we could apply for work visas was an experience we will never forget. In a lightning-speed span of only forty minutes, we managed to have blood and urine tests, chest X-rays, ultrasound, vision testing, and a general medical examination. It took me a lot longer than that to figure out how to work the washing machine because the instructions were in Chinese characters!

After a few meals of cold tinned peaches, we mastered the gas and cooked rice for dinner. I was grateful to have a hot shower.

During our first week of work, we toured the orphanages and the hospital we would work at. We were keen to take our boys into the orphanage so they could see firsthand why we had upended their lives and left grandparents, school friends, and soccer and swimming lessons to come to a city on the other side of the world.

The first room we walked into was filled with about twenty babies. Many had cleft lips and or palates. The boys were initially horrified to see these deformities, but not long after we arrived, the boys won the hearts of the babies with the stuffed koalas (finally someone liked them). The children sat or stood giggling at the crazy foreign visitors who not only looked funny but made funny sounds and faces too!

When it was time for us to leave, the babies howled. Thomas and James clung to me, pleading to go back into the nursery. "Can we go back in? They want us to go back in. I think they may be lonely." I dragged the reluctant boys away. It was hard to leave the crying children, knowing that all they wanted was to be picked up and cuddled.

The orphanage we worked with had a caregiver-to-child ratio of one to five, which was excellent, yet each caregiver had to prepare meals, wash and fold clothing and cloth nappies, and do all the cleaning. Caring for five young babies is hard enough, but in addition, feeding one baby with a cleft palate can take up to forty minutes every three hours! It certainly doesn't leave much time for cuddles, singing lullabies, and playing games.

That day was our first experience of many of how hard life was for children in the orphanages.

As I tucked the boys in bed that night, said a prayer, read a book, and sang a song, I couldn't help but think of that room with twenty children who, despite being well fed and clothed, had no Mum or Dad to tuck them in every night. We prayed for these children who often had no one to listen to their cries and prayed that one day they would have a family to call their own. Meanwhile, I encouraged the boys that we needed to trust in God and His promises to us. And to them!

'He does not ignore the cry of the afflicted.'

—Psalm 9:12

Over the next month we gradually settled into a routine of home schooling—I taught maths and english; Sam taught music and physical education—and work. I typically performed medical clinics at the orphanages, and Sam worked at the clinic in town, attending to foreigners and Chinese patients. Everyone seemed happy with the arrangement.

On my first day of work in the orphanage I saw a dear little boy named Oliver. I wrote about him in my journal about six months later:

It was my first day of work in the orphanage. After the hour and a half bus ride, standing cramped between an old lady and a middle-aged man who smelt strongly of garlic and cigarette smoke, we finally arrived at the orphanage, an impressive building to the north of the city.

I unpacked my medical bag and wondered who my first patient would be. I was expecting to see the abandoned healthy girls I had heard and read so much about. To my surprise in walked my first patient, a four-year-old boy with a scar above his right eye. His English name was Oliver. He was a gorgeous little boy with a mischievous smile. He sat on my lap whilst the nurse and translator talked about him rapidly. His story stunned me. Six months earlier he had been left on a street corner by his beloved father, who had told Oliver he was going to get some lunch and be right back.

He never returned.

Poor Oliver had stood for hours on that street corner until someone took him to the police station, where he was reported as an abandoned child. He was then admitted into the local orphanage.

He had a tumour behind his eye, which was slowly growing and distorting his eye. We assume it was because of this that his parents had made the decision to abandon him. They may have feared not being able to care for him. It may have been shame that he was disfigured and would not be accepted in the Chinese community, where keeping face is so important. Or it may have been that they were a poor family who couldn't afford any medical care, certainly not an operation! But we will never know for sure why they left him on that street corner. Either will Oliver.

Whatever the reason, this little boy who should have been or possibly was a cherished member of a family, had now become an orphan.

Under the new Tomorrow Program, the Chinese government pays for all necessary operations performed on orphans, so Oliver would get the operation he needed to remove the tumour. Did the family know that before they relinquished him? Had they deliberately given him up so he could receive the medical care they couldn't afford?

I can't help but wonder what I would do if Thomas and James were in the same situation. Could I make the choice never to see my own child again in exchange for their health and a chance at life?

I can't help but wonder what Oliver and his parents' last night together was like. Tucking a child into bed, knowing this is my last night with him would break my heart. The last story! The last song! The last good-night kiss and the last, "Sleep well. I'll see you in the morning." For tomorrow morning is the last time I will see the child I have loved for the past three years.

I can't help but wonder how those parents felt on the last morning. If it were me, my son would wake up happily like every other day. He is eager to have his rice porridge for breakfast and then have a day filled with fun and adventure like every other day. But I know it's not just another day. Today is the day he becomes an orphan and I lose a child.

I would go through the morning routine of breakfast with a false smile on my face, getting dressed and cleaning the dishes, pretending today is just an ordinary day, yet knowing that tonight he and I will be heartbroken as we spend our first night of forever apart.

Could I do what tens of thousands of Chinese parents do every year? I have heard and read too many stories of the heartbreak these parents suffer at abandoning their children.

Many hide and follow the child to make sure he or she is safe. Was Oliver's Dad hiding behind a building somewhere, watching his precious son crying and searching for his beloved 'Ba Ba'?

Fortunately for Oliver, the tumour was benign and described on CT scan and at the operation as a 'fatty lump.' He was left only with a droopy eye and a small scar. Unfortunately for Oliver the removal of this fatty lump, which would probably be an overnight hospital stay in the Western world, had rendered this little boy an orphan. Due to the strict law against child abandonment in China, his parents will never be able to reclaim him.

Over the following six months I have seen his little face many times, and every time his eyes looked a little sadder and his smile less mischievous. He stopped asking when his Dad would come and get him and stopped running up to strangers for a cuddle.

Sick and alone in a hospital bed, at the orphanage Christmas party and crying when having blood tests, he will never again know the comfort of his mother's arms. He now knows that his family will never return for him.

I can only pray that one day his sparkle will return when he is adopted into a loving family. And I pray that he knows the truth of this verse:

> *'Though my father and mother forsake me, the* L*ORD* *will receive me.'*
>
> —Psalm 27:10

Little Oliver's story was the first of many sad stories I would hear over the following years. Every time I heard a story like his, my heart would break for the parents and the child. I felt so helpless. I have gradually learnt to turn my sadness and frustration into prayer, and I pray that these children will be received and loved by the Lord and one day by adoptive families.

'As a mother comforts her child, so will I comfort you.'

—Isaiah 66:13

One night Sam had a dream in which he witnessed our house in Australia burning to the ground. In the dream we all stood back and watched as it vanished in flames before our very eyes.

The next morning, he woke, shaken by the dream and the mental picture of watching our house of ten years disappear. He felt strongly that this was more than 'just a dream brought on by too much spicy food.' He felt that God was challenging him and speaking to him through it. "Would you sell your house for me?" he felt God asking. "Would you give it all up to help people in China?"

To both of us that was a hard call. Our house was full of memories: bringing Thomas and James home as newborns to their newly decorated bedrooms. Building the cubby house and the sandpit. Sitting on the balcony overlooking the water, and having barbecues with friends. I loved our house. Not because it would win any 'home beautiful' awards, but because it was our home where I saw Thomas start kindergarten, James walk and talk, and where we first dreamed of our 'China girl.'

Sam was less attached to the house. To him it signified security rather than memories. We received no pay from our work in China. The rent we received from our house in Australia was our only income. And our home gave us a sense of comfort in knowing that there was something to fall back on if times got tough.

We both spoke about how we would cope if we felt God calling us to sell the house and use the money for work in China. Would we be like the rich young man Jesus spoke about in Luke 18:18–23, and go away sad because we couldn't part with our money and possessions? Or would we be like the widow who gave away everything and trusted in God - 21:1–4?

We decided that we would have to pray and trust God that, if the time did come, we would be able to put God and His service first before our own wealth and comfort.

Julie Mallinson

'With man this is impossible, but with God all things are possible.'

—Matthew 19:26

Chapter Five

Viruses, Milk Scandals, and Earthquakes

Some people believe that tragedies occur in sets of three. Although I don't ascribe to such superstition, our first few months in China did seem to support it.

It was 2008, the year of the Beijing Olympics. We constantly heard, "I love you, Beijing" and "Beijing welcomes you" being sung through strategically placed loudspeakers in the supermarkets, parks, and on the crowded buses, yet we didn't feel excessively welcomed.

First, there was the hand, foot, and mouth disease (HFMD) scare. A killer version of this usually harmless virus was spreading throughout China at an alarming rate. A number of children had died and many were in intensive care with heart failure as a result.

I was thankful that my children were isolated in the almost sterile home school environment. I thought that this scare was a justifiable reason to catch taxis rather than buses. Being crammed in a small bus with up to one hundred people was the best way to catch such viruses, and so I convinced my ever frugal husband to avoid buses and crowds in a bid to avoid infection.

So the scare didn't really affect me until I visited the orphanage to perform a medical clinic. Every second child was suspected of having HFMD, and I realized that institutionalized living, not riding on buses, was the best way for this virus to disseminate.

I nervously donned my gloves and attempted to look confident as I examined these children, constantly thinking and praying that these kids wouldn't be infected and, more important, that I wouldn't transfer the virus to Thomas and James.

Fortunately, they were all free from infection, and as the weather gradually warmed, the number of infections dwindled.

Soon after this the milk scandal was upon us. Milk had been adulterated with the protein melamine so that it appeared to have a higher protein content. As a result, a number of deaths throughout China occurred and countless other children were admitted into hospitals with kidney stones and renal failure. Eleven countries worldwide, including Australia, banned importation of Chinese manufactured dairy products; however Australians living in China couldn't avoid such products.

In our city, foreigners and locals alike were concerned regarding the potential effects on their children, as it was primarily children who succumbed to the effects of tainted milk. Fellow foreign doctors in China reassured us that we needn't worry unless our children drank large quantities of milk. Unfortunately, I had been making the boys milk shakes three times a day - at least! With the difficulty in obtaining breakfast cereal or wholemeal bread, the boys were constantly hungry, so I was trying to satisfy their ever increasing appetites with what I thought was healthy milk!

Overnight, what I deemed was a healthy and easy treat had become a potential poison. So the daily intake of chocolate and strawberry milk shakes and an afternoon iced coffee for an exhausted Mum were abruptly ceased. We were back to snacking on rigorously sterilized fruit, rice bars, and good old tinned peaches.

The milk scandal demonstrated to me that no matter what lengths I went to, I couldn't completely shield my children from all the potential hazards in China. Or in Australia, for that matter! Despite never eating street food, sterilizing our hands multiple times a day, and washing fruit in an elaborate number of steps, including soaking in diluted bleach, I still couldn't ensure that they lived in a safe little bubble. I really had to entrust them and our safety in China to God.

This lesson I slowly learnt and am still in the process of learning. How do I find the healthy balance between overprotecting my children and trusting God with the health and safety of our little ones? How tight do I hold their hands when crossing the road? How many times do I sterilize our fruit? Should they eat street food? How do we avoid the potentially rabid dogs? Do all mosquitoes in China carry Japanese encephalitis?

Even in Australia I questioned my ability to keep the boys free from any dangers: Can they really ride a bike to school alone? Do I trust them and their friends to make wise choices when searching on the Internet? Can they really go to a pool party? Without me? Without a life jacket? Are we sure there aren't sharks in that water?

I gradually learnt to entrust the care of the children to the almighty Father, who created them and loves them even more than I do.

While it may break the heart of a wise parent, they realize that it is not love to shelter a child from every adversity and all hardship.

It is through occasional adversity and the winds of life blowing against us that we develop the muscles to stand strong and steady, gaining our moral balance.

Katherine Walden, I Lift My Eyes Ministries (http://psalm121.ca/)

Three weeks after arriving in China, my ninety-year-old grandfather's health deteriorated. He died on Mother's Day 2008. He was much loved by us all and left my grandmother a widow after over sixty years of marriage. Mum rang to inform us of the news but also to let us know that Great Pa, as the boys affectionately called him, quoted the whole of Psalm 121 just hours before his death. We were all encouraged to know that in his final days he could lift his eyes to the Maker of heaven and earth for comfort and peace.

'I lift up my eyes to the hills–
where does my help come from?
My help comes from the LORD,
the Maker of heaven and earth.
He will not let your foot slip–
He who watches over you will not slumber;
indeed, He who watches over Israel
will neither slumber nor sleep.
The LORD watches over you–

the LORD is your shade at your right hand;
the sun will not harm you by day,
nor the moon by night.
The LORD will keep you from all harm –
He will watch over your life;
the LORD will watch over your coming and going
both now and forevermore.'

—Psalm 121

Great Pa had always been an important part of our lives. I wanted to return to Australia for his funeral and to support my Mum and my grandmother. So that night as Sam madly researched possible flights, I settled the boys in bed and explained to them what had happened and what our plans were. I spoke to them about Great Pa and Psalm 121, and together we searched through Psalms to find a suitable verse to encourage and support my Mum and nan.

I remember glancing at Psalm 46; my favourite, Psalm 139; and of course the famous Psalm 23, but nothing seemed more applicable than Psalm 121, the one Great Pa had quoted himself. So I tucked the boys in, said a quick prayer and then started packing for the unexpected trip home.

The next day dawned to become a lovely China spring day. We spent the morning haphazardly packing bags and our home schooling supplies, and then after lunch we ventured to the local supermarket to buy goodies for the flight— chocolate and snacks.

The shops were busy as usual. Every day in a Chinese supermarket is like Christmas Eve in an Australian one. In the world's most populated country, personal space is not as important as it is in Australia, so just to get through the front door and up the escalators is a mammoth effort and a lesson in assertiveness. We pushed and shoved our way past the masses of shoppers to the second floor to look for some clothes for the boys to wear back in Australia.

Five minutes of clothes shopping was enough for Sam and the boys, so they quickly deserted me in search of something more exciting—the electronics aisle. We arranged to meet downstairs in fifteen minutes; however, they returned five minutes later, unfruitful in their search.

Seconds after their return, we noticed the store signs swinging. People started screaming and scrambling for the door. The ground began swaying and buckling at an alarming rate. Earthquake! Panicked, we grabbed the boys' hands and ran for the emergency exit, dodging tumbling bikes and toys and fending off boxes that were flying off the shelves and bouncing on the floor around us. We survived the crowd crush escaping down the stairs. Finally making it into the street, we found ourselves surrounded by what seemed to be millions of Chinese people screaming and crying.

We made our way to a local park and sat on a hill overlooking the polluted canal that surrounded the city. Huddling together, we asked one another if we were okay. Sam had inadvertently escaped from the supermarket with a block of chocolate he'd been holding just as the quake hit, so with shaking hands we all took a piece, then surveyed the chaos around us.

We had no idea how extensive the earthquake had been, whether to expect aftershocks or if people had been killed. The power was out, so we had no way to get news reports from television, radio, or Internet. To be in an earthquake is a terrifying experience, but to be in one in a foreign country where you don't speak the language is even more frightening. We felt even more isolated in the midst of horror.

Once we had all calmed down a bit, we explained to James that no, we were not returning to the supermarket to retrieve his Spiderman shoe he'd lost in the rush. Our next task was to get ourselves home. Of course, we weren't sure what condition our apartment was in or if it was even still standing. To this day, I still don't know if the shaking I felt on the way home was aftershocks or my shaking legs.

What would normally have been a walk of a few minutes turned into a hike of over an hour. We had to get around the rubble that hindered our way. The roads which were usually packed with cars, trucks, buses and bicycles all impatiently beeping their horns were eerily quiet. The footpaths, usually crowded with eager people trying to sell us their wares, were now crowded with the local residents. People who had fled from their apartments during the quake lined the streets. If it wasn't so scary it would have been funny to see all these people milling around in their pajamas! Many were smoking, munching on sunflower seeds, and chatting casually, completely at ease as if the earthquake was of no consequence!

The number of disabled people lining the streets surprised me. Older people sat propped on makeshift piles of blankets and pillows, but also with them were many disabled younger people whom I had never seen before. Children and teenagers with what appeared to be cerebral palsy, limb defects, and developmental delay seemed to be enjoying the sunshine, completely oblivious to all the fuss.

I discovered later that many people are embarrassed and ashamed of their or their family members' disabilities so they stay indoors most of the time, venturing out only under cover of darkness so the disability is not so noticeable. Of course, even the shame of being disabled was not as powerful as an earthquake, so they came out of hiding for safety's sake.

We arrived home to find our ground-floor apartment intact. We shakily gathered around the kitchen table. The boys were brimming with questions I could not answer. Why do earthquakes happen? Would there be more? What happened to the underground workers or those in trains at the time?

As Sam patiently explained to them the details of tectonic plates and fault lines, I recalled my search through the Psalms the night before, in particular Psalm 46.

I opened to it and hoping to sound calm and in control read it to the boys:

> *'God is our refuge and strength, an ever-present help in trouble. Therefore we will not fear, though the earth give way and the mountains fall into the heart of the sea, though its waters roar and foam and the mountains quake with their surging.'*
>
> —Psalm 46:1–3

We prayed and thanked God that He had kept us safe amidst the quaking mountains and earth giving way. I wondered how many people hadn't been as lucky as us.

It was not until we arrived back in Australia forty-eight hours later that we were able to learn more about what we had experienced. We were stunned to learn that the 7.9 magnitude earthquake was dubbed the 'Great Sichuan earthquake' the deadliest earthquake to hit China since 1976, killing more than 70,000 people and rendering up to eleven million homeless. Many children died in the quake. Poor quality school building was blamed for many of these precious souls were in school when the walls collapsed on them. My heart broke for the countless families who had lost their precious only children. The government later announced that these families were 'allowed' to have another child as a replacement, with no fines or penalties incurred. Maybe it was a case of too little, too late for these families.

Trying to sleep the night of the earthquake was impossible, for in my mind I relived all we had experienced that day. And then the interminable 'what ifs' threatened to crush me. What if one or both of our boys had been killed? How would I cope? What if our boys had been in a school that day? What if they were trapped under the rubble for hours, even days? What if the boys and Sam hadn't returned to me just seconds before the earthquake hit? What if we hadn't been preparing to return to Australia, and instead Sam would have been at work and the boys and I would've been home? How would we have coped for hours apart with no public transport or communication to tell each other we were safe?

"What if?" My mind repeated to itself multiple times that night, as we all slept fully dressed in anticipation of aftershocks.

Surprisingly there were no aftershocks that night. It was as if the earth got all its fury out in one mighty belch. Thankfully the airport re-opened early the next morning so we were still able to board our flight to Australia. And twenty-four hours later, we were back on Australian soil. I breathed a sigh of relief as the wheels hit the tarmac. We were safe! No more earthquakes, killer viruses, or poisoned milk. I was home!

A few days later, I sat in familiar comfort on my parents' balcony, surrounded by the familiar sounds of kookaburras and lorikeets. I picked up a book from the many well-read and loved books on my Mum's bookshelf—Corrie ten Boom's The Hiding Place. My mind was open to understand what Corrie meant when she wrote: "There are no 'if's' in God's world. And no places that are safer than other places. The center of His will is our only safety—let us pray that we may always know it!"

Over the next few weeks and months as I remembered the earthquake, my mind would once again wander to the 'what ifs.' But instead of following that line of thought, I remembered and clung to Corrie's wise words.

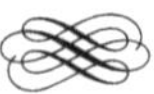

We spent three weeks in Australia: attended my grandfather's funeral, caught up with family and friends, and stocked up on necessities we missed in China, such as coffee, vegemite, hand sanitizer, and blue-tack.

We encountered difficulties in obtaining a work visa to return to China. It was the year of the Olympics in Beijing, and fewer foreigners were allocated work visas due to perceived security threats. Because we weren't associated with a large company or business, it was hard to prove that we had good reason to be permitted to return to China. We filled out multiple forms, made many phone calls, and produced photos to prove who we were, but still we were unsuccessful in obtaining work visas.

One morning I travelled to Sydney with the boys to once again apply. We left the Central Coast at 5AM, taking buses, trains and taxis to arrive at the Chinese consulate by opening time at 9 AM. It was crowded and chaotic as usual. I heard disgruntled people in front of me as their visa applications were denied.

Finally, it was our turn to face the lady at the counter, disapproval written all over her face. We too turned away disappointed as she denied the visa for some unexplained clerical reason.

Tired, hungry, and greatly dejected, the boys and I shuffled out onto the bustling Sydney street. Immediately the boys barraged me with questions.

"What are we going to do?"

"Why are you upset?"

"When can we go home?"

"What are we going to have for lunch?"

"I'm upset because we can't go back to China. We know that God wants us to go back there but we can't." I failed to keep my frustration in check. Even to my own ears, I could hear the irony that I believed the

God of the universe was going to be thwarted by the details of a visa application.

We walked to the closest corner store, a dingy shop packed with all sorts of food, and we bought a hearty lunch of chips, chocolate, and soft drink.

We slumped on the steps, and as the boys munched their snacks, I read my Bible, once again hoping for some divine inspiration. The words I read seemed just for me as I sat tired and disappointed on those dirty concrete steps.

> *'Let us not become weary in doing good, for at the proper time we will reap a harvest if we do not give up.'*
>
> —Galatians 6:9

Determined not to lose heart, I hustled the boys aboard the train for the long trip home. Our stomachs were full of food and my heart was full of the resolve to trust that the God who had prepared good works for us in China would help us reach our destination.

After several more applications and trips to the Chinese consulate in Sydney, we eventually were granted a tourist visa, which would allow us to stay for another three months and apply for a work visa within China. It wasn't ideal, but at least we were able to return to China as planned. So in early June, once again with bags bulging, we boarded yet another flight and returned to China to continue our work there.

Soon after our arrival in China, we sat in the Chinese visa office, bringing with us additional photos and filling out more forms. As we waited for our paperwork to be processed, I entertained the boys with games of hangman and noughts and crosses. Sam began chatting to a lovely man also awaiting his visa approval. On conversing with him, Sam discovered that he was a Pakistani medical student studying in China. Sam shared with him our faith and hope in Christ and the reason we left comfortable and prosperous Australia for a country where Christianity was frowned upon and life was often not so comfortable. This man listened closely to all that Sam said.

I marveled at how God would place us in a situation where we could witness to a Muslim in the visa office of a Communist country. I certainly had never envisaged such an opportunity, which never would have occurred had we received our work visa in Australia.

We left the office with our work visas and the added blessing of a lifelong friend who has great respect for Sam, his wisdom, his Christianity, and his medical knowledge. This man is now home in Pakistan. He regularly emails us and asks us to pray for him, his family, and his country.

> *'Many, O Lord my God, are the wonders you have done. The things you planned for us no one can recount to you; were I to speak and tell of them, they would be too many to declare.'*
>
> —Psalm 40:5

Chapter Six

Tupperware Family

Arriving back in China felt almost like coming home. Even though we had been there for only a short time, we were the only foreigners in our small community and known by everyone. The fruit and veggie sellers, neighbours and guards at our gate were all friendly and seemed happy to see us again.

The warming weather brought green grass and a profusion of cherry tree blossoms. Our short time in Australia had refreshed us and we were feeling positive about settling into our familiar routines.

We got to know one family who lived in the bike shed. There seemed to be grandparents and countless young children living in a small room within the bike parking area. Our boys enjoyed playing with the boys of similar age, and Thomas and James never failed to return home wide-eyed at what they had experienced.

Thomas and James reported how the four children and grandparents would share a bed in a room smaller than our bathroom. They would cook, do homework, and even clean their teeth outside. One time they had found an old watermelon in the rubbish, only half-eaten. So with great excitement, the kids took turns carrying it back to their grateful grandparents.

I realized that this was the family I'd heard about who made a living from recycling. They weren't quite homeless, but almost. Their 'home' had no real walls or door, rather pieces of cardboard roughly attached to the fence to give them some privacy and meager warmth during the freezing winters.

One day I rummaged through my Tupperware drawer and discovered many lidless containers and other odds and ends that had doubtless been left there by the previous foreign volunteers. I collected all of the lidless containers in a big bag and deposited it beside the rubbish bin. Either by China's poor design or God's special design, our kitchen window looked directly onto the rubbish pile. So I saw the little two-year-old girl discover the bag and excitedly call out to her grandfather. Almost immediately, she was surrounded by her grandparents, older cousins, and older sister. The joy on all their faces was like the boys' on Christmas day. With eyes shining they unpacked the goodies that the 'rich foreign lady' had discarded.

After that, we enjoyed throwing out our recyclable goods and seeing how this thrifty family could use it. They would take bottles, jars, used schoolwork, even broken pencils and bring new use to them. The days we threw out an old McDonald's toy or the free Qantas travel pack were particularly exciting.

Not long after the earthquake we noticed that they had a new baby girl. The family's love and adoration for her was obvious. She would often sit in a recycled pram as her grandmother sang to her while she cooked dinner. We still hadn't seen the parents of the children and assumed that they were out working or, as may have been the case of the mother, resting indoors after giving birth.

I wrote an email to friends and family back in Australia and told them all about this family we had dubbed the 'Tupperware family.' People were moved with compassion and soon little gifts of clothing and toys arrived for them. One group donated a beautiful quilted blanket for the new baby. With the assistance of a Chinese speaking friend to translate for us, we eagerly took the gifts to them. It felt good to give them something brand-new for a change. We explained that the toys were for the older children and the blanket for their new baby.

"This isn't our baby," they said, as the grandmother prepared a bottle for her and the grandfather held her proudly. "We found her on the garbage pile after the earthquake. She was crying and cold so we thought we should look after her."

I was dumbfounded . . . not to mention humbled.

Here was the poorest family I had ever met, and they had willingly taken on another child who was not their own. They had loved her, clothed her, and fed her like she was theirs.

I thought back to the many conversations I'd had with people regarding adoption.

"We can't afford to adopt because we have just built a pool."

"We don't know if it is fair as there wouldn't be enough bedrooms for all the kids to have their own."

"We' don't know how we would afford to send all the children to university."

This family, without a thought regarding their own belongings or lack thereof, had seen a need and responded. That she needed food, love, and a family to them replaced any adoption and fostering training and overcame any financial obstacle.

I was amazed at God's perfect timing at engineering such circumstances to occur right outside my kitchen window. For there was another little girl in need of a family who would take her in and love her without doubts or questioning. Could we extend unconditional love and 'recycle' a child just like the Tupperware family did? Could we cheerfully greet the needy with smiles and love just as they did? Could I live out the truth in the verses I read and knew but often didn't act upon?

> *'For we brought nothing into the world, and we can take nothing out of it. But if we have food and clothing, we will be content with that.'*
>
> —1 Timothy 6:7–8

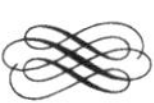

Over the next few months we settled deeper and more comfortably into life in China. We developed a semi routine between sharing the workload and teaching the boys. We made some great friends and the boys enjoyed the onset of warmer weather so they could play outside on their bikes. I had managed to work out the shopping, cooking, and buses. Sam worked out how to watch football online. We had enjoyable family days exploring local parks, shopping at the markets, and watching the boys run through fountains . . . to the dismay of many local onlookers.

But some days were not as pleasant and carefree as others. Some days the spelling words seemed to be impossible and the boys were reluctant students. Some days we would barely see any patients at work, and the children at the orphanage seemed to have an overwhelming number of problems, both medical and social, that I could not cure.

One day Sam and I slumped onto the lounge in the heat, exhausted by another day of seemingly fruitless work and frustrating home schooling. "Why are we here? Is it worth it?" Sam lamented.

"We were helping more people back in Australia—at least we could make money and support the needy in China," I complained.

As I juggled home schooling, work, shopping, cooking, and cleaning, the 'glamour' of living and working in a foreign country faded and the reality set in. After working years in a busy medical practice, volunteering at the school and church, and meeting friends for prayer and encouragement, I felt that now I was doing nothing. Sam felt the same. In Australia he would see at least forty patients a day. It was hard to get used to seeing only three or four here in China.

One day I read the verse: '*God is not unjust; He will not forget your work and the love you have shown Him as you have helped His people and continue to help them*' - Hebrews 6:10. But was I doing what was considered good? Was I helping anyone? I couldn't see how researching one hundred easy dishes to cook with rice, or teaching Thomas the silent K rule was benefiting anyone. My time was filled with home schooling and house chores. I rarely felt I had an opportunity to show love to others, and I certainly didn't feel like our decision to move to China was helping anyone.

A few days later I read Ephesians 2:10: '*For we are God's workmanship, created in Christ Jesus to do good works, which God prepared in advance for us to do.*'

I felt comforted that somewhere, maybe just around the corner, there were good works for me to do that God had prepared for me in advance. I just had to trust and wait . . .

Little did I know that the events over the next few months would change the course of our focus in China and make us so busy that some days we wished we had less to do!

Another Camp

In early July we packed our bags and headed off to our second 'Bring Me Hope' summer camp, which was situated outside the city of Nanchang, one of the hottest cities in China, evidenced by the 30 degrees celsius temperature when our plane landed at 7 AM!

This year we were attending the full four weeks as staff and were excited to meet more kids and to help facilitate the children, their foreign volunteers, and translators form bonds that would change the lives of all attendees.

Anticipation marked each Monday as we wondered what the new group of orphans we would soon meet would be like.

Exhilaration filled Tuesdays and Wednesdays as we watched these children grow in confidence as they experienced love for the first time.

Despondency threatened to overwhelm Thursdays and Fridays as we prepared for the inevitable good-byes we'd have to say to these children and send them off to an unknown future.

It was an emotional roller coaster and an exhausting one at that. The staff kept our energy boosted with large amounts of iced coffee, prayer, and the knowledge that this would be something that would alter orphan care forever. We saw lives changed as translators heard about God for the first time, volunteers witnessed the plight of the orphan and went home energized to help them in any way they could. Children smiled and laughed, basking in the knowledge that finally they were special to someone.

Whilst at camp we answered the occasional email from work in Xian. Many foreigners had deserted Xian in a bid to escape the oppressive summer heat, so no medical clinics were organized. We intermittently received an email from someone wanting to know which antibiotics to use and the schedule for the next village doctor training that Sam was organizing. Apart from that, all of our energy and attention was focused on the camp.

Until our last week in Nanchang!

During that last week of camp, we received an email from one of the orphanages our company was associated with. One of the children had just been discovered to be HIV positive, and the staff was petrified of the effect it would have on them. They had been told by doctors that they needed weekly blood tests to determine if they had contracted the virus from the child and only time would tell. They all assumed that they had automatically contracted the virus.

There was also the fate of the little girl. No one was willing to look after her so the orphanage was stuck with a child with no caregiver.

Through email we tried to allay fears as much as we could and promised that on our return to Xian we would visit the orphanage and talk to the staff about their concerns. Meanwhile, our Chinese coworker contacted an American HIV specialist who lived in Xian whom she had met on a medical trip to the earthquake ravaged Sichuan area. He promised to give us medical advice and inform us if there was anything we could do to help this little girl.

To be honest, the fate of this single child two provinces away seemed far removed from the daily grind of meetings, setting up for craft, organizing meals for sixty people, and all the other responsibilities of camp life.

Upon return to Xian, we struggled to settle in after the emotional and spiritual highs of camp. That we were back in our two-bedroom apartment in an area with no other foreigners hit us hard. Thomas especially struggled and would cry every night as I put him to bed, telling me daily how lonely he was. He couldn't communicate with the other boys in our neighbourhood, and even if he could, they were never available to play, as they were often at school and tutoring until nine o'clock at night. Even the kids from the Tupperware family were often too busy to play.

One day I was feeling particularly sorry for him and guilt ridden about dragging him away from Australia and everything he knew and loved. He had come and said, "Mum, how do you ask someone to play with you in Chinese?"

I didn't know.

That night he cried and said how much he missed his camp friends and his family and friends back in Australia. I slept fitfully and worried about what the future held for us and in particular the children. It seemed reasonable for us to make big decisions and sacrifices for God and China, but was it fair on the kids? Was it all worth it when our kids were lonely, missing out on soccer, friends, and swimming lessons, not to mention risking killer viruses, milk scares, and earthquakes? It seemed to me that the heartache and risks were currently outweighing any potential benefit. I know the boys felt it too. I vowed that I would do all I could to make the China experience a good one for them.

The next morning dawned like any other. Home schooling, cooking, and cleaning. During our lunch break the kids and I went to the company office to collect the mail. We always looked forward to this little break in home schooling, not only because we passed a bakery selling hot bread rolls filled with apricot jam, but also receiving mail was always exciting. We looked forward to the goodies we would often receive. Friends would send me coffee, chocolate, books, and other treats. The boys groaned and rolled their eyes whenever school work arrived but would soon rummage through the package, looking for the library books their teacher had sent.

This day there was no coffee or chocolates but a single letter from Australia, a card from my Mum and an article she had cut out of a magazine, written by Naomi Reed, author and missionary in Nepal. (The Presbyterian Pulse , 2008)

The article was entitled 'But What about Our Children'? Naomi described exactly the emotions I was struggling with. "It's the question that keeps us awake at three in the morning. God may be leading us to Mongolia or Iraq, Nepal or Kazakhstan . . . But what about our children?" Her opening questions grabbed my attention after my night of poor sleep.

"How will they cope? Will they make any friends? What if they get sick? Will they turn out alright?"

She wrote about the many fears we parents have but also that evidence shows that these children who have been raised on the mission field have become 'adaptable and empathetic adults with a highly developed world view.'

She finished the article with this: "And then one night in some far distant country, we'll wake up at three in the morning and smile, knowingly profoundly that He who holds the sparrows has a plan for our children. He who numbers the hairs on their heads also knows what tomorrow holds. And then we'll slowly lean back on our pillow . . . and find rest."

As I finished reading the article and drained my cup of tea, I watched the boys. They were happily making towers and roads for their cars, oblivious that their mother was spending so much time and energy worrying about them! I felt reassured that I was not the only Mum who woke at 3 AM worrying about her children. God, who cared for them, also cared for me enough to reach down and give me the perfect article at the perfect time.

Some months later I wrote in my journal on the subject.

One of the hardest things about being a foreigner is worrying about what we are 'doing to' our children. I somehow conveniently forget that God called us to come to China and He knew we had children!

I worry about pollution, terrorism and lead poisoning, Meningitis, abduction, and food poisoning.

I am slightly comforted knowing that I am not the only Mum who feels this way. My Christian friends and I often sit around talking about our children.

We wonder what we are doing to our children. We forget to talk about what He is doing to our children.

Recently, Thomas, aged nine, went to buy some toys with his foreign friend. They had been saving their pocket money to 'buy up big.' On the way home from the shop, the recently purchased toy broke, which is sadly too often the way in China. Thomas's friend was understandably angry and threw the toy to the ground in disgust.

Thomas piped up. "You know, if you were a Chinese orphan you would still love that toy, because they don't have any toys."

My heart swelled with pride when I heard that story. Not only has God been faithful and protected Thomas from all the evils I feared, but He has protected and nurtured his heart into one filled with empathy and compassion.

I am no more able to protect Thomas from lead poisoning than I am able to change his heart, yet God can do both.

I have spent so many hours praying, "Keep him safe on the roads, cure his cough, and protect him from evil." But I also need to remember to pray, "Give him a heart full of love for You, give him a passion for You and helping others, and give him a heart of flesh not stone."

> *'Are not two sparrows sold for a penny? Yet not one of them will fall to the ground apart from the will of your Father. And even the very hairs of your head are all numbered. So don't be afraid; you are worth more than many sparrows.'*
>
> —Matthew 10:29–31

Chapter Seven

Finding Pearl

Later that week we packed our bags, spelling lists, stethoscopes, and mosquito repellent and travelled to the village of Hanzhong.

Chinese staff and foreigners alike had told us how pleasant it was to escape the city and experience life in the countryside. They assured us that the pace of life was relaxed. Even the thought of Japanese encephalitis–carrying mosquitoes didn't deter us from looking forward to the adventure.

We were surprised to discover on arrival that this 'country village' was the home to over two million people! Another reminder that China is the most populated country on the planet.

After the four-hour bus trip winding through the beautiful Qing Ling Mountains, we settled into the two-bedroom apartment, our home for the week.

I unpacked our few clothes and converted the dining table into a school room. The boys excitedly ventured outside to the shared courtyard and kicked their new soccer ball around. They were quickly surrounded by a crowd of Chinese children who found their white skin and blue eyes quite the novelty.

Later that evening we meandered down the street for dinner, hoping to eat just across that road where we had previously spotted many brightly decorated Chinese restaurants. Much to our dismay, Hanzhong was not as Westernized as Xian, where all the menus included pictures of the dishes. Here none of the menus had pictures. Instead, the waitress handed us a dirty, stained piece of paper covered in Chinese characters, which was completely illegible to us.

We tried the random point-and-guess technique of ordering our food. We were rewarded promptly with a plate of cold grey food that looked alarmingly like worms! But we figured that it could have been worse. Sam had only recently been served pigs ears to munch on; however, despite our hunger after the long journey, none was willing to eat what we later identified as cold, pickled eggplant. We instead decided, much to the boys' relief and joy, that KFC would be the one-stop shop for all our culinary needs. So every evening that week, this family of foreigners caught a bus to go downtown for yet another piece of fried chicken!

That night, with stomachs full of chicken, chips, and sundaes, we slept soundly, wondering what tomorrow would bring.

On our first day in Hanzhong, we planned to visit the orphanage and train the staff regarding HIV. While we worked with the staff, the boys would meet and play with the children, which they always loved doing. Seeing firsthand the work we were doing helped the boys appreciate the reason for our being in China.

So on day one we set off for the orphanage. We passed wagons piled high with building supplies and drawn by large, tired-looking horses. We were happy to leave the dusty, noisy city behind and drive through fields of rice paddies. Within ten minutes we arrived at a dirty run-down little village. Chickens running loose on the road squawked at us and stray dogs cast menacing stares our way. James huddled on my lap for protection.

Dao le, the taxi driver, announced, "We are here." I wondered if he was lost or confused (or both), as this certainly didn't seem the right setting for an orphanage. But as we clambered out of the cab, a teenage boy with cerebral palsy opened a gate. Indeed we had arrived!

The first item on our agenda was to attend the meeting to discuss the fate of the little girl with HIV and how we would train the staff to care for her. We sat with volunteers and Chinese staff in a cramped, hot, and humid room and gratefully sipped iced coffee that one of the American volunteers had made for us. The orphanage was surrounded by rice paddies, which only added to the sense of suffocation in the room. Mosquitoes buzzed both inside and outside the room, and I tried not to imagine what diseases they were carrying.

Thomas and James played outside as we sat and discussed the recent events and the need to establish an HIV protocol.

Through our translator we managed to understand recent events. The child in question had arrived in June, a month after the earthquake. She was frail and malnourished and suffered from severe diarrhoea and vomiting over the ensuing weeks. She seemed to be hungry all the time, screaming almost constantly. Despite her hearty appetite, she continued to lose weight. She was admitted to hospital and a CT scan revealed an enlarged bowel. It was decided then that she needed an operation. During the pre-op workup she was diagnosed with HIV. A single blood test had changed her life forever.

And ours!

She was then quickly transferred back to the orphanage, whose staff was told by the doctors that they could do nothing for her. It was only a matter of time for this little girl. Upon her return to the orphanage, accompanied by the diagnosis, all thoughts of her welfare and impending death were cast aside as the staff had panicked, questioning how the disease would affect them? Had they contracted HIV as well? How long did they have left to live?

Most of the caregivers were convinced that they had contracted HIV in the preceding weeks and were terrified. All of the caregivers refused to touch this increasingly frail little girl, and she certainly wasn't allowed to be with the other children for fear of spread. One caregiver had agreed to take her to a group home where a single Mum cared for seven children. The child, named Pearl, would live in this group home temporarily, whilst her fate was determined by the orphanage staff.

My wonderful friend, Natalie, who was one of the only foreign volunteers at the orphanage, wrote about Pearl's time in the orphanage: "I remember when Pearl came to us. Up till then I had seen many children who had passed away due to being extremely sick, and when I saw Pearl, I knew she was dying. I thought she would not live very long. One day I changed her nappy. She was so thin that the skin on her body hung off of her legs and arms. She was constantly hungry, and once she saw food she would cry until she was given it. Pearl had no way to keep any food or nutrients in her body, she either threw up everything or had diarrhoea. No matter what I would do, she did not smile.

Every morning when I arrived at the orphanage, Pearl would be sitting outside in her pram with a doll. She did not show any expression in her face. The house mama would often put her outside in the pram. Even though she was the only house mama out of all them to even go near Pearl, I think deep down inside she was terrified that she too would get HIV. She asked me one time if she could get HIV from breathing the same air as Pearl. I told her she could not. I do not know if that is why Pearl was outside a lot. I had a baby body carrier that I put Pearl in sometimes so that I could hold her while I was doing work and bring her around with me. I was sad that others were too fearful to hold her. I could not tell if Pearl liked this or not. She had only two expressions—she either cried or had a blank look."

How long could her life go on like this? How long would she live? What would happen in the freezing winter months when she couldn't be left outside in the pram?

Her fate was a big question mark.

Our translator stated as calmly as if she was giving us the time of day that the orphanage director had twice suggested that Pearl be placed in a storage room and allowed to die. The problem would then be well and truly off their hands. Even the hospital where the doctors diagnosed her condition shredded all medical notes pertaining to Pearl. If this plan were followed, there would be no record that she had ever existed.

As they offered this option for her demise, I felt physically sick. My heart raced within my chest, and sweat, not from the oppressive heat, broke out across my forehead as I heard with my own ears the evil that man so easily devises.

Having medically cared for many children and adults, I know too well that people, even children, die. But for anyone to sob to death from hunger, thirst, and loneliness in a storage room must be one of the most terrible ways to depart this world. I couldn't help but think back to a paper I had written about the needs of dying children in an Australian hospital. These children were loved, held, sung to, and comforted until they took their last breaths. We couldn't stop the dying, but we could provide presence and comfort along the way. How different it would be for this little girl in a sweltering hot room in central China!

Sam and I were overwhelmed by the needs regarding training, reassurance, and even medical care that were presented at this two hour meeting. What could two Australian general practitioners do? We had a total of about four hours training in HIV, and as a medical student in a Sydney teaching hospital I had seen only one patient with HIV. I certainly hadn't learnt how to train and reassure a whole community, let alone care for a seriously unwell HIV positive child.

At the end of the meeting Sam suggested that we visit the patient and take photos of us and the boys touching and holding her. We could then display these photos around the orphanage to help dispel the fear. It was also suggested that we offer one-on-one counseling and medical advice to any staff who requested it due to their contact with the child.

So the boys, Sam, and I set off for the group home in question.

The orphanage consisted of three large two-story buildings. They were joined together by rather old-looking concrete. An odd tree or shrub was visible in a pot beside the buildings. The playground, complete with a slide and climbing frame, was empty of children due to the searing heat and that the children and staff were having their midday rest.

As we approached the home, a dear little boy ran out to greet us. He jumped all around us and screamed for joy as he eagerly tried to share his apple with us. Thomas and James pulled out a stuffed koala and kept him entertained whilst I looked around the stark but clean room.

The house mother spoke in Chinese to our translator as I took in the small kitchen, well-polished floors, and rooms off the lounge room, each with two or three bunk beds. This was my first time in such a group home, and I was pleasantly surprised at how clean and well organized it was. It was devoid of the usual clutter of toys, books, and snacks that usually littered my lounge room, but the children looked well clothed, clean, and fed.

"There she is." Our translator interrupted my daydreaming and pointed to an ugly, wasted child sitting mournfully in a pram. I was sure that this child was a boy. The group mother reassured me that this child with a shaved head and big sorrowful eyes was indeed the child who had been named Pearl by an American volunteer.

The staff agreed to my request to pick her up. Immediately after I lifted her scrawny body from the pram, she laid her head on my shoulder. Her tense body relaxed at once and the caregiver pointed out all that this girl wanted was to be held by someone.

As I sang 'Jesus Loves Me' to her, I noticed that she had a garbage bag over her cloth nappy, and I could feel every bone in her body. While I held her and sang to her, Sam took a medical history from her caregiver and reassured her that she would not catch HIV caring for her.

Sam snapped several pictures with his camera as I held her and the boys talked to her. I usually avoid at all costs having my picture taken (just ask my Mum), and this day should have been no exception. I was tired, hot, and certainly hadn't done my hair and makeup! But I let Sam take photos so we could display them and use them for education purposes.

As we prepared to leave, I gently set her back in the pram, almost afraid that she would break. As soon as she left my arms, she commenced wailing and looked back at me pleadingly. The boys spoke to her, held her, and touched her, intrigued that such a frail little thing could make so much noise!

That afternoon we left Pearl and the other children and headed back to the city for our dinner of KFC. After another hearty meal of fried chicken, I made an entry in my journal.

August 2008

"There she is. Her name is Pearl," someone says and points to a child in a pram, sitting forlornly away from the other children.

We have seen so many children who seem well loved and cared for and have some hope for the future and a forever family. But this child has no one. Who is her advocate? What will become of her?

> *'Surely the arm of the Lord is not too short to save, nor his ear too dull to hear.'*
>
> —Isaiah 59:1

Over the next few days, Sam and I alternated in working at the orphanage and home schooling the boys. We were kept busy examining children with heart failure, hydrocephalus (which should have been treated with an operation but hadn't been), and cerebral palsy. We also saw nearly twenty staff members who feared for their lives because of their contact with Pearl.

We patiently reassured them that their concerns regarding their contact with her—feeding, nappy changing, and dressing—would not give them HIV. We assured them that no one had ever 'caught' HIV from daily living with another HIV-infected person. We told them that urine, sweat, tears, and feces weren't infective and certainly touching and holding the child would not put them in any risk.

We learnt that Pearl had a constant cough and was at risk from pneumocystis carinii pneumonia, one of the most common causes of death in people with HIV. We could prevent it with antibiotics—a cheap and simple antibiotic that is used all the time in Australia, England, and America—but not as easily found in China.

On our last day in Hanzhong, the orphanage arranged for a driver to take me searching for the needed antibiotic. Armed with the Chinese medical dictionary and a piece of paper with the antibiotic name scrawled on it, we visited every pharmacy and hospital in the city looking for the simple but vital medication.

I was surprised by the vast array of antibiotics and medications they supplied. Antibiotics and combinations that I had never heard of, not to mention all the Chinese herbal preparations I was offered; however, the one antibiotic I needed was nowhere to be found. I returned home defeated and frustrated but feeling that I had done all I could.

That night, after what was thankfully our last meal at KFC for a very long time we sat together and watched the Olympic closing ceremony on TV. Despite all the hype and rumours the Beijing Olympics had finished successfully, and China had superbly hosted this prestigious event to the surprise of many critics. We sat mesmerized by the performance as time after time China impressed the world with its skills, people power, and creativity. I couldn't relax and truly enjoy it, however, without thinking that in the very same country was a little girl who would likely die a terrible death because we couldn't find the correct antibiotics or blood tests to help her.

'You hear, O Lord, the desire of the afflicted; you encourage them, and you listen to their cry, defending the fatherless and the oppressed, in order that man, who is of the earth, may terrify no more.'

—Psalm 10:17–18

Chapter Eight

What Does the Lord Require of Us?

We returned home changed people. Again!

Not only because of our encounter with Pearl, but also because of all the other children who we had met. Earlier we had applied to foster an orphan during the weekends, and I was hoping and praying that little Oliver, whom I had met on my first day at the orphanage, could spend weekends with us whilst he awaited his forever family. I imagined how much fun he would have playing cars and riding bikes with two big brothers.

Sam and I began to pray for the future and especially for the good works that God had prepared for us. I wondered if I should do some work with palliative care. Caring for dying orphans seemed to be such a huge need. Meeting Pearl reinforced to me how much these children needed love and medical care in their last days. I had also heard about the lack of pain relief given in China. There seemed to be a real fear amongst doctors to prescribe analgesia, and using strong medications like morphine was almost unheard of.

Sam and I wondered if we should think about adopting a special needs child. We had never seen a healthy girl in the many orphanages we had visited. We did notice, though, that the orphanages were brimming with special needs children who needed a family to care for them and love them. It was extremely difficult to adopt a special needs child into Australia, but we'd heard some rumours about a special needs programme starting.

I looked forward to finishing school work at two in the afternoon and then sitting in the sun with a cup of tea and my prayer journal. Being isolated from family and friends and the normal hectic life in Australia made me spend more time in prayer. Over the next few weeks I sought God's direction for our lives and asked Him again and again why on earth we were in China.

They boys had no swimming lessons, I did not meet friends for coffee, nor did I have any church meetings or play dates. Even cleaning a two-bedroom apartment didn't take much time, and getting the washing done wasn't an ordeal since the boys insisted on wearing the same clothes for a week. I certainly didn't have school uniforms to iron.

So I sat and sipped tea, read the Bible, and wrote out my feelings, hopes, struggles, and prayers. I have years of prayers written in well-worn A4 books. I had begun writing my prayers down as a way to keep my mind upon Him rather than on my own needs. All too often I would start praying and end up planning what to cook for dinner, worrying about what to wear the next day, and thinking of all the housework that needed to be done.

Often I flick back through my prayer journals and I am always encouraged by how God heard and answered my prayers. Over my time in China I had written many pages of prayers. Some scrawled almost illegibly in the middle of the night; some written neatly as I sat in a Western-style cafe, sipping coffee; and some written from my bedroom during the kids' lunch break. I also kept a record of the Bible verses and quotes that particularly encouraged me and spoke to me.

I love looking back on the weeks surrounding our meeting with Pearl, recalling my response to her and feelings about her, and seeing how God faithfully answered every one of those prayers. Interspersed with complaints about the difficulties of living in China, prayers for friends for the boys, and prayers for friends and family back home, I also wrote prayers for this little girl we had met briefly but who had remained on both Sam's and my heart.

Thanks to Sam's continued persistence, two months after we met Pearl she was transferred to an infectious disease hospital in our city to commence investigations and treatment for her now end-stage HIV. She had lost even more weight. At eighteen months she weighed less than 6 kg. Her CD 4 count placed her in the most severe HIV category, but miraculously she had not contracted pneumonia or another life-threatening infection.

I jotted my thoughts when she was transferred to our city.

October 14, 2008

"Thank you, Lord, that Pearl was able to come to Xian. I continue to pray that your Spirit leads us and guides us so we know what we should do to help orphans. Help lead me as to whether we should start a hospice for orphans."

October 15, 2008

> *'Defend the cause of the weak and fatherless; maintain the rights of the poor and oppressed. Rescue the weak and needy; deliver them from the hand of the wicked.'*
>
> —Psalm 82:3–4

I came to my quiet time today wanting to be led by Your Word about Pearl and how we can help her. Should we foster her?

The words in Psalm 82 confirm to me that this child is precious to You, loved by You, and yes, You do want us to care for her in whatever way we can."

October 17, 2008

"I pray that You guide me in what we should do regarding adoption. Help Sam and I to clearly know what path You want us to choose?? Special needs?? Adopting within China?? Thank You for preparing a child for us in advance, and surround that child with Your love and protection."

October 24, 2008

"Lord, I pray for Pearl in the hospital. I pray that You give us wisdom in her management and that You would be a comfort and strength to her. I pray that she is loved and happy and not too confused. Help lead us and guide us in how we can help her."

It seemed like our prayers had been answered. The amazing medical team at the infectious disease hospital investigated Pearl extensively and had commenced her antiretroviral HIV medication treatment.

Her diarrhoea and vomiting settled down and she was eating happily. To us it seemed that the story was over as hospital staff prepared to send her back to the orphanage with medication. But at the end of October, Sam came home, his body and face tense with bridled fury. "The orphanage won't have her back! Even though she is on medication and we have trained the staff, still no one will care for her."

I sank onto the chair at our kitchen table, disheartened by the futility of all our hard work. "It seems like she is falling through the cracks of the system." I spoke gently, trying to console Sam.

He paced the small room, running his fingers through his hair. "She is being pushed through the cracks!"

Those who know Sam know what a patient, kind, and tolerant man he is. When I lose the car keys multiple times and the kids misbehave on a long plane flight, when he faces irate, drunken patients in the middle of the night, and when others criticize him or expect too much of him, he would always react calmly. I would often joke that it was like being married to Pollyanna. He always saw the good in everyone and every situation.

But that day we saw a side of Sam that surprised us, the righteous anger of someone witnessing a huge injustice and not being able to do anything about it. Sam's favourite Bible verse had always been Micah 6:8: 'He has showed you, O man, what is good. And what does the LORD require of you? To act justly and to love mercy and to walk humbly with your God.'

I could see that he was struggling with the call for justice yet being powerless to do anything about it. As a man, he always wanted to 'do something to fix it', but now all he could do was sit and watch as others made one wrong decision after another.

My mind returned to the verse in Psalm 82 calling us to rescue the needy from the wicked. But how could two foreigners in China do this? It seemed an impossible call. Politically, medically, financially, and practically, there didn't seem to be anything we could do for this little girl.

The next day, October 25, 2008, I read a verse that spoke to me clearly about the situation we were in.

> *'Rescue those being led away to death; hold back those staggering toward slaughter. If you say, 'But we knew nothing about this,' does not he who weighs the heart perceive it? Does not he who guards your life know it? Will he not repay each person according to what he has done'?*
>
> —Proverbs 24:11–13

How could we stand by and watch as this child was left to die? How could we say we didn't know what was happening, when we had heard with our own ears the plan they had for her? How could we do nothing, when we'd held her in our own arms? Sam and I talked long into the night and agreed that if another family or caregiver didn't come forward, we would short-term foster her until a solution was found. Long-term fostering was out of the question, because we would be returning to Australia in six months and could never adopt her.

For the following week, our company staff continued to negotiate with the orphanage and looked for a caregiver or family willing to care for Pearl. Sam and I continued to pray for her. I prayed on October 30, "Lord, please be with Pearl and us. Help us know what You want for her and the plans You have for her. Help us find a caregiver for her and a family to look after her. Help us know what is best for her." Whilst we prayed and waited, little Pearl was still in the hospital, awaiting test results and for someone to care for her.

During this time, we learnt that Chinese hospitals function different from Australian ones, in that all the care of the patient is given by the family. Food, toileting, washing, and even the administration of medicine are all done by family. No wonder when Chinese people get admitted to a hospital in Australia the whole family moves in!

As you can imagine, caring for a sick child in hospital while juggling work commitments, the care for other children and tending to aging parents who often live in the family home is an arduous task. But who would attend to hospitalized orphans' daily cares?

In this case, the orphanage staff are responsible. However, in Pearl's case there was no one willing, so we organized a roster of twenty-four hour shifts for the staff at the small clinic where we worked. Although nervous about Pearl's HIV, they were willing to risk themselves for her sake. Sam gladly put himself on the roster and spent Sunday, day and night, caring for Pearl in the hospital. He wrote about his experience to our family, friends, and supporters back home.

"My heart belongs to someone else!!! Yesterday, I left my family, and she and I spent all day together . . . eating, relaxing, laughing, watching Real Madrid play Juventus! What a day—one I will never forget!

She is nineteen (months), an orphan, and suffering from HIV. After much pleading and persistence, she was finally allowed to come to the hospital, be tested (confirm her diagnosis—quite advanced now), and have her treatment started. Even though her life will be short, she knows the 'quality of mercy' dropping like gentle rain from heaven.

Our team here has been giving her twenty-four hour care while in hospital. I am so proud of them.

Fear is still the driving force which will have most people avoiding even a simple touch . . . but our team has the knowledge and the compassion to make a difference in this child's life.

She is precious.

My prayer is that her life . . . her illness . . . and her care can change and soften the hearts and minds of those who come in contact with her."

To tell the truth, the boys and I were a bit put out that someone seemed to be as important to Sam as we were. We wondered what was so amazing about her.

We were soon to find out.

Julie Mallinson

'Is not this the kind of fasting I have chosen: to loose the chains of injustice and untie the cords of the yoke, to set the oppressed free and break every yoke? Is it not to share your food with the hungry and to provide the poor wanderer with shelter—when you see the naked, to clothe him'?

—Isaiah 58:6–7

Chapter Nine

The Least of These

Exactly one week after he wrote that email, we received a phone call at 10 PM on a Sunday night. Our company director told us what we had been expecting but hoping not to be true. No one would care for Pearl. She was being discharged at 8 AM the next day with nowhere to go.

"Will you look after her?" she pleaded.

"Yes!" We didn't hesitate.

People tell us how amazing and brave we were in making that decision. But that night we both made a decision that we knew was God's will. Over the previous month He had been speaking to us and encouraging us not to ignore her cries and suffering. He had beseeched us to 'defend the cause of the weak and fatherless' and He had even given us the 'Tupperware family' as neighbours to show us unconditional love and acceptance. How could we sit by and quote

'*God sets the lonely in families*' - Psalm 68:6 when we weren't willing to be one of those families? How could we praise Him as the 'father of the fatherless' when we, his 'hands and feet weren't willing to risk our own comfort to care for one of the 'least of these?'

That night we went to bed in perfect peace, knowing that tomorrow morning this little girl would have a home (albeit temporary) and a pillow on which to rest her head on the following night.

On the day Pearl arrived, Sam and the boys busily went shopping. I am sure the local shop owners who knew us well enough by now, began to wonder what was going on as they watched Sam, Thomas, and James making multiple trips back and forth, laden with baths, sheets, baby food, and prams. The only thing missing was a baby!

Hours later it was obvious that they were shocked to see the foreigners sporting a new malnourished Chinese baby. Even the Tupperware family seemed to be amused at the shopping procession and the subsequent arrival of a frail, miserable Pearl.

I reluctantly went to work that day, knowing that when I came home a little girl would be in our midst. It was hard to concentrate on seeing patients, teaching our Chinese doctor, and looking up Chinese drug names on the Internet when I would rather have been home with Sam and the now three kids.

I came home six hours later to a house full of laughter, nappies, baby bottles, and mess! The boys loved their new 'sister' and delighted in making her laugh at their crazy faces and antics with blocks.

"Look, Mum, she can smile." And they again and again made towers fall, tickled her feet, and blew bubbles for her to pop with her boney hands.

Any family who has adopted will know the absolute joy it is to see the first smile on a previously withdrawn and lonely orphan. God must smile in heaven every time He sees it.

Her first bath initially frightened her. But Pearl quickly settled into the warm water and enjoyed splashing for what was probably the first time in her nineteen months of life.

She was overjoyed to be given an unlimited food supply and happily drank her formula, munched on meat sticks, rice, and noodles. She quickly learnt where the food was stored, and although unable to walk or even crawl, she could point at the kitchen cupboards and scream until they were opened!

That night we made a makeshift bed on the floor out of blankets and suitcases. She drifted off into a contended sleep with me at her side.

> *'I will lie down and sleep in peace,for You alone, O* Lord,*make me dwell in safety.'*
>
> —Psalm 4:8

Day two was not so easy. We were moving into a new apartment in just four days, and I was amazed at how much 'stuff' four people could cram into a two-bedroom apartment in less than six months. The next few days passed in a chaotic blur, but at the end of the week I snatched a few precious moments to reflect on our first week with Pearl.

This week we took in Pearl a nineteen-month-old orphan with HIV.

We took her not because we are brave, heroic, or even loving, but because she had nowhere else to go. The future for her in an orphanage was bleak, if not nonexistent. If she did survive she would always be isolated and deprived of affection and love because people fear her disease so deeply.

On the first day at home with her, I tried to pack for our upcoming move and home school the boys. I certainly had no time to bond with this little girl as I rushed around, giving her medicine, packing boxes, and trying to supervise my reluctant school students, who would rather play with the newcomer than read their books. Pearl, however, decided to bond with me, despite the fact that I had broken every rule in the fostering and adoption books. Despite repeated attempts to settle her at her rest time, she would not sleep unless I was by her side. Every time her eyes shut, I would creep out of the room. But sensing movement, those big brown eyes would fly open and see that I was not with her. She'd start wailing again. Finally I gave in and lay down with her until she gave in to sleep.

Now that she was asleep, I had some time to get things done. What should I do? Clean the house? Pack another box? Teach the boys? I was exhausted and beginning to have second thoughts about the wisdom of adding another child to our already chaotic lives. I decided to ignore all the temptations to 'do something' and sat amongst the mess with a strong cup of tea and my Bible. The study that day was on Matthew 25.

> *Then the King will say to those on his right, "Come, you who are blessed by My Father; take your inheritance, the kingdom prepared for you since the creation of the world. For I was hungry and you gave Me something to eat, I was thirsty and you gave Me something to drink, I was a stranger and you invited Me in, I needed clothes and*

> *you clothed Me, I was sick and you looked after Me, I was in prison and you came to visit Me."*
>
> *Then the righteous will answer him, "Lord, when did we see you hungry and feed you, or thirsty and give you something to drink? When did we see you a stranger and invite you in, or needing clothes and clothe you? When did we see you sick or in prison and go to visit you?"*
>
> *The King will reply, "I tell you the truth, whatever you did for one of the least of these brothers of mine, you did for me."*
>
> —Matthew 25 vv. 34–40

Tears streamed down my face as I read these words. I realized that God was speaking to me and showing me how much he valued Pearl and what we were doing for her.

We had fed her, given her clothing, and invited her in, even though to us she was a stranger. It never crossed our minds that what we did for her, we were actually doing to God. 'The least of these' was lying on my bedroom floor, yet the King of the universe was reminding me that what I was doing for her, I was actually doing for Him.

God had seen my doubts, my tiredness and frustration and He clearly spoke to me that afternoon to remind me that what I was doing was not in vain.

> *'Do not forget to entertain strangers, for by so doing some people have entertained angels without knowing it.'*
>
> —Hebrews 13:2

The following week we continued to pray and search for an appropriate family. We weren't convinced that we were the best family for her. We seemed to be caught in a catch-22 situation. If she died it would be terrible. But if she lived we couldn't keep her. Whatever happened, she couldn't be with us for long.

On one hand, we weren't sure what her prognosis was. She had only just commenced antiretroviral treatment, so only time would tell if she would respond. The thought continued to niggle at me that she was unlikely to survive the six months until her second birthday.

We were fully prepared to care for her and give her a loving home and a peaceful death, but how would that affect our boys? How would it affect us to lose a girl who within a week had stolen all our hearts with her cheeky smile and mischievous sense of humour?

I selfishly struggled with how I could love a child and become attached to her, knowing I would lose her. Even as I struggled and prayed about this, I knew that I was daily becoming more attached to her and her to me.

A friend sent a poem to help me and encourage me, and as I read it again and again I tried to convince myself that this didn't apply to our situation.

God's Loan

"I'll lend to you for a little time,
A child of mine," He said,
"'For you to love the while she lives
And mourn for when she's dead.

It may be six or seven years
Or twenty-two or -three,
But will you—till I take him back—
Take care of her for Me?

She'll bring her charms to gladden you
Though her stay be brief.
You'll have these precious memories,
As solace for your grief.

I cannot promise she will stay
Since all from earth return.
But there are lessons taught down there
I want this child to learn.

I've looked this whole world over

In My search for teachers true,
And in the crowds that throng life's land,
I have selected you.

Now will you give her all your love
Not think the labour vain,
Nor hate Me when I come to call
To take her back again?"

It seems to me I heard them say,
"Dear Lord, Thy will be done.
For all the joys Thy child shall bring,
Though pain will surely come.

We'll shelter her with tenderness,
We'll love her while we may,
And for the happiness we've known
Forever grateful stay.

And should the angels call for her,
Much sooner than we've planned,
We'll brave the bitter grief that comes
And try to understand.
Anonymous

—Edgar A. Guest.

The poem reminded me that all of our children are special loans from God and that I needed to love, nurture, and enjoy them but not suffocate or cling to them. I knew that despite her illness and probable death, God had entrusted her care to our family.

On the other hand, if Pearl did miraculously respond to medication, what would happen to her then? As Australians we were unable to adopt special needs children from other countries, and I was pretty sure that HIV would be high on the special needs list. So a Chinese foster family or an orphanage that accepted HIV-positive children seemed a solution that would be hard for us in the short-term but the best for her in the long-term.

Despite hours of searching, we were unable to locate any family or orphanage willing to care for her. We were beginning to discover how huge the fear of HIV is within China.

Again and again, our Chinese staff told us that no one would take her knowing her illness. Again and again, they warned us to be quiet regarding her illness, because if locals found out we would quickly be evicted from our apartment. Again and again, they told us that we were the best place for her.

Finally, two weeks after her first night on our bedroom floor, our Chinese orphanage director found an orphanage in a far distant province that would accept her. Instead of feeling relief, Sam and I felt only sadness.

Already she was waking up with a smile and loved stroking my hair as I carried her to the table for breakfast. She loved her pink clothes and soft toys, and she kissed and hugged them and held them closely at bed time. She loved her brothers, being tickled by them, and playing with cars, bubbles, and crayons alongside them.

The thought of putting this child in an orphanage with no brothers to play with, no songs and cuddles from Mum, and no piggyback rides from Dad was something that neither Sam nor I could entertain.

So, despite that we had no idea what the future would hold for any of us, Sam emailed the orphanage and politely declined the offer:

"Julie and I and our family have become quite attached to little Pearl and would find it very hard to see her go to another orphanage. I realize we probably have little or no say in what happens to her care, but we would prefer that she stays in a family—be that ours, or another. She is flourishing so much with family love.

Maybe we can discuss this further face-to-face when we are there.

Thank you for the love I know you feel for her too.

We would keep her for as long as God has given her to us for, whether it be three, 23, or 63 years.

'All the days ordained for me were written in your book before one of them came to be.'

—Psalm 139:16

Chapter Ten

Living with Lazarus

The following two weeks with Pearl were drama-free. We somehow managed to move house and she happily settled into our routine. The boys loved her, and she rewarded us all with smiles, giggles, and cuddles.

I daily walked to the shops with my two blue-eyed boys and Pearl in a baby carrier strapped to my front. Not many nineteen-month-old babies have the luxury of being carried this way, but being less than seven kilograms, she was the size of a six-month-old.

With Pearl in tow I received a lot of attention. Chinese grannies surrounded me. They'd poke and prod and offer advice. I understood less than 10 percent of what they said but clearly understood their gestures as they pinched her tiny legs and shook their heads disapprovingly. I am sure they wondered why this foreign woman was caring for such a malnourished child. Pearl's spindly legs were further evidence that the Western diet was inferior to the Chinese one!

Despite spending three months in an orphanage with minimal physical contact, I was convinced that she had been loved by someone—probably her biological Mum. When changing her nappy she would automatically put her hands up to me to be carried and she would settle happily to sleep as long as she could see me. When I held her, she would pat my back or stroke my hair. She'd learned these physical gestures from someone.

Many orphans who have never had physical comfort don't know how to self-soothe. They will often hit their heads against the cot sides and will not know how to anticipate or be soothed by physical contact. I was convinced by her actions and the way she settled into our family so easily that Pearl had been loved before.

Studies have shown that children who have formed a bond once can more easily bond a second time- far easier than those children who have never bonded. Despite the grief of losing a primary caregiver, the physical and emotional attention the child received benefits his or her future emotional and psychological health.

We took Pearl to our local church—a collection of foreigners meeting in an apartment. She quickly became popular and loved to be held and cuddled. She delighted in being the focus of attention. Her favourite part of the service was communion. As soon as she saw the bread, she jumped up, eagerly hoping she would be given a morsel.

Three weeks after joining our family, I was holding her at church and innocently handed her to Sam so I could collect our belongings. The screaming that ensued sounded like she was being tortured.

There began six months when Pearl's behaviour told the whole world that she was a Mummy's girl. Whenever I wasn't in view, she would become extremely distressed, screaming at the top of her lungs. Bedtime was particularly hard as she would scream "Mama!" for at least an hour every night. Once she learnt to crawl, she added banging on the door to her repertoire. This quickly exhausted our whole family, and probably the neighbours as well. To allay her fear, I lay with her every night and sang her to sleep.

Well-meaning friends suggested letting her cry herself to sleep. After two kids, and one a particularly bad sleeper, I considered myself somewhat an expert in letting children cry. But what about this child who had likely watched her Mum walk away, abandoning her on a street side? What was Pearl thinking when I left her room? Was she scared that I, too, would leave her? How could I let her cry herself to sleep if she thought my leaving was permanent? Was it even possible that 'controlled crying' would work with Pearl?

I had read about the 'honeymoon period' with adopted children. Often orphaned children settle into family life well and smoothly and the family breathes a sigh of relief, thinking that this whole adoption experience is easier than they thought. But a few weeks later, the children realize how much they now have and how much they want someone to love them, care for them, and respond to their every need. Often an intense period of separation anxiety follows.

I decided to stay with Pearl until she settled. No matter what her future held she needed unconditional love and to know that I was there for her.

The process took a lengthy six months, and we had some very long nights. By the age of three Pearl had heard 'Here I Am to Worship' so many times that she could sing it by heart. I was also afforded many hours to pray and ponder her future and past as I lay beside her.

Gradually she grew stronger in confidence and happier that we would not leave her.

Every book, every group, and every person has a different theory on how to deal with orphaned children. Pearl showed us that no matter how much head knowledge you may possess, you have to be led by the child and what you feel is right for them. Our reward for hours of prayer and patience was a happy, loving little girl, but I am fully aware that this is not the case for many adoptive families. God only knows how we can protect the hearts of these little ones who have already experienced abandonment, heartbreak, and rejection. The best we can do is to surround them in prayer and remember that their tears mean more to their heavenly Father than we can imagine.

> In my distress I called to the LORD; I cried to my God for help.
> From His temple He heard my voice; my cry came before Him, into His ears.
>
> —Psalm 18:6

Six weeks after she joined our family, Pearl became unwell with a high fever. Normally we would just monitor a child with a fever and make sure it was simply a viral illness, but with such a poor immune system, we knew we had to act fast.

Despite feeling terrible and too weak to even eat or drink, she continued to reach out for me as we prepared for her probable hospital admission. This time we knew to pack food, drink, clothing and even toilet paper. Sam would be her caregiver within the hospital, so he would be unable to leave her side to replenish his supplies.

An hour after becoming febrile, she sat on Sam's lap as they hurtled in a taxi to the infectious disease hospital. He was weighed down with a tearful little girl and bags bulging with instant noodles, baby food, bananas, and toiletries.

Pearl was admitted immediately and underwent a series of investigations, X-rays, TB tests, CT scans, and more.

Though this was Sam's second experience of living in a Chinese hospital and he was more prepared than the first time, it still surprised him that he had to buy her medicine from the local pharmacy to help with her fever. It seemed that high-dose intravenous antibiotics were included in the price, but a small dose of oral paracetamol was considered a luxury!

Pearl improved overnight. All tests came back clear, so we suspected that she had contracted a virus. Her hospital admission wasn't futile, however, because the staff had remembered her from her first admission—when she was close to death—and they were astounded that she had gained weight and looked so healthy.

On the second day of Pearl's hospital stay, a medical professor appeared on his ward round accompanied by many trainee doctors and registrars. As Pearl sat on the bed playing with her pink Hello Kitty phone, he lectured them all loudly in Chinese. Sam noticed that all were sheepishly looking at their feet as the man spoke quickly, pointing to Sam and Pearl. Fortunately a friend of ours was present, and after the doctor and his students left, he explained to Sam what had been said.

The Chinese Professor of Medicine was berating himself and his fellow countrymen for not standing up to care for children such as Pearl. He continued to say that this was a Chinese child but her fellow Chinese had refused to help her and instead it was foreigners who took up the challenge. This was the first but certainly not the last time we heard such sentiments from the Chinese. People would often give me the thumbs-up when they saw us with Pearl, and even the Chinese church thought it great that the foreigners wanted to help such children. I tried to remind them that we were not helping them because of our nationality but because we were Christians—adopted and loved by God, who spurs us on towards love and good deeds to others. 'He predestined us to be adopted as his sons through Jesus Christ, in accordance with his pleasure and will' (Ephesians 1:5).

As a good friend once said, the hardship we face as we go through adoption and fostering these children is nothing compared to the hardship Jesus suffered so that his Father could adopt us.

Pearl came home to us a few days later, and we were all so happy to have her back. The house had been quiet without her, and the boys and I had missed her constant presence and destructive influence on our home schooling days.

I was so pleased that the Chinese doctors had been able to see the miraculous improvement love, prayer, and antiretroviral therapy could cause in a little girl on the brink of death. I was grateful that she was being prayed for all around the world.

As the boys settled back to their studies, I penned a quick email to friends and family back home.

> "Hi All,
> Thanks to everyone who has emailed us and been praying for Pearl.
>
> She was unwell for the first day but then awoke the next morning with no temperature and demanding food!! (Always a good sign.)
>
> She has had multiple investigations and was initially going to be in for a week, but I just got a call that if she remains well overnight, she will come home tomorrow.
>
> Her admission and time in hospital has been an interesting experience in healthcare here. (BYO food and even medicine.)
>
> It has also been an amazing testimony.
>
> The director of the hospital was so amazed to see the change in her over the last five weeks that he got all the medical students into the room and told them how impressed he was that a company like ours would care for the lowest of low. (Being an orphan with HIV is even one step lower than being an orphan.)
>
> We were really glad that he and the hospital staff could see what a difference that our BIG company, the head of which is

the 'father of the fatherless' - Psalm 68:5, has made in the life of this little girl!

Love,
Julie"

Sam and I both hoped and prayed that this would be the first of many times that her life would give glory to God and hope for other orphans suffering with HIV. 'Declare his glory among the nations, his marvelous deeds among all peoples. For great is the LORD and most worthy of praise; he is to be feared above all gods' (Psalm 96:3–4).

Over the following six months Pearl responded dramatically to her antiretroviral medication. The child we thought would live only six months started crawling before Christmas and walking the month after. Her face and body filled out. It was hard to believe that this chubby-cheeked toddler was the same scrawny girl we had taken in a few months prior.

We began training people (including ourselves!) about HIV.

Transmission, Response to Medication, Prognosis.

HIV was first discovered whilst we were at medical school, so we had little formal education regarding treatment and prognosis. We were surprised to learn that Pearl's prognosis was good, according to the 'Lazarus' effect, a situation in which patients are so unwell that they seem to be dying, yet with proper medical treatment they improve over a few weeks' time. We certainly witnessed a Lazarus in our home!

We spoke to a few friends who were HIV specialists and heard how whole villages in Africa were changed when those at death's door miraculously responded to treatment. We also learnt that, sadly, less than 47 percent of those requiring this lifesaving treatment actually received it.

Again and again I would remember the dramatic photos I had seen on TV and in magazines. I remembered mothers holding a wasted baby, dying with AIDS. Mothers watching helplessly as their children continue to lose weight, succumbing to infection before slipping away into eternity.

I tried not to put myself in their position, but because Pearl had been one of those frail, lifeless little children only six months prior haunted me. I couldn't begin to imagine what it would be like to go back to that stage.

Pearl turned two in March. A milestone we never expected to achieve. We hosted a combined party for her and James, who turned six a week later.

Unlike most foreigners, I had no lessons in speaking Mandarin. Nearly a year after we had arrived in China I was still struggling to get by with my minimal language skills. With Pearl's arrival and home schooling the boys, trying to learn a new language was quickly delegated to the back burner.

I braved ordering James's favourite chocolate mousse cake at the local bakery. Much pointing and sign language later, I managed to explain the cake I wanted and even confirm the day and time of pickup. They gave me a pen and paper and spoke to me rapidly in Chinese. I wrote my name and phone number on the paper and headed home, relieved and secretly quite pleased with myself.

The next day dawned. I made fairy bread and cleaned the house. Many foreigners were coming, so I decorated the house and prepared for our game of pass the parcel. All I had to do was pick up the cake. I proudly walked to the bakery, congratulating myself on my ability to order it so successfully. As I approached the bakery window, I spotted the large cake on display with JULIE MALLINSON 85403035 written on it in white chocolate! Ahhh . . . the pencil and paper were for me to write the message I wanted on the cake, not my name and phone number!

I walked home, protectively carrying the cake that announced to the world that I could not speak Chinese.

The party was a great success, with only a few good-natured remarks about the "Julie Mallinson" birthday cake and Sam kindly pointing out "It's not all about you." The boys both fought over being the one to eat JULIE.

It was one of the few occasions that living in a non-English-speaking country was funny. Usually, battling with the language and cultural differences was frustrating and demoralizing. I had somehow gone from a well-known local doctor giving talks at Rotary and church functions to a crazy foreigner who couldn't even manage to order a birthday cake.

After the birthday cake debacle, I thought it might be worthwhile after all to take some Chinese lessons. I was brave enough to take only one lesson a week, enough to help me know left and right and maybe even successfully order a cake for next year.

I had a lovely Christian teacher and we enjoyed each other's company. I took pleasure in the lessons and tried to chat to her as much as I could in a strange mixture of Chinese and English. I figured that the more aimless chatting we did, the less of the grammar and pronunciation we would have to do, not to mention writing characters, which to my pragmatic brain seemed a colossal waste of time and effort.

She was patient with me and kindly accepted my weekly excuses of being too busy to do my homework. She punished me once for complaining about being tired. I had to sing (unaccompanied) a psalm in Chinese. It's hard enough for me to sing one in English, let alone Chinese!

I never complained again.

I gradually began to tell her about Pearl. She was always interested in knowing what new mischief Pearl was up to. I nervously even told her about the HIV. Upon recovering from the shock, my teacher proceeded to ask many questions. "Don't you think you will get it? Aren't you scared for the boys? How long will she live? Does she have medicine? Is she sick all the time?"

Upon reassuring her that no we were not scared, that Pearl was often the healthiest member of our family, and that she had a good life expectancy, we would settle down to pronunciation, grammar, and even writing characters, much to my dismay.

My teacher's name was also Pearl. One day she shared how she came to have that name. "My first English teacher gave me the name Pearl. She said that a pearl is something that starts off small and ugly, but through lots of hardship and with the hand of Jesus becomes something beautiful."

What a perfect description of any Christian but especially our Pearl, who had started off as an unlovely, unwanted piece of sand and evolved into our precious jewel.

A pearl is a beautiful thing that is produced by an injured life.

It is the tear [that results] from the injury of the oyster.

The treasure of our being in this world is also produced by an injured life.

If we had not been wounded, if we had not been injured, then we will not produce the pearl.

Stephan Hoeller.

Chapter Eleven

Help! I'm an Alien!

The weeks and days passed as we continued to adapt to our Chinese environment. Some days seemed to last forever as we battled the language, pollution, different foods, and culture.

Some days the cultural differences were funny: Babies wore no nappies but "split pants"; we learnt not to step in puddles in the elevator. The challenge of eating with chopsticks; we learnt how to say spoon in Chinese.

Some days we enjoyed the differences. We all loved watching the women dancing in the park, old men playing Mah Jong on every street corner, and eager school students following us around, saying, "Hello. Nice to meet you." One of our favourite places to eat was at the local Kao Rou restaurant, where we balanced on tiny stools as we feasted on many, many pieces of barbecued meat. As I discovered how delicious street food actually was, I began to relax on my previous resolution to avoid it!

The boys were happy that we didn't wear seat belts and that the five of us could easily squeeze into the back seat of a taxi. James, at one stage, even wished we were Chinese. A Chinese friend offered him a ride on the back of his bicycle. Before his ever-cautious mother had time to object, the then five-year-old James plonked unceremoniously on the makeshift child's seat on the rear of the bike.

No seat belt.

No helmet.

James had the ride of his life as the boys wove precariously through the five lanes of traffic on the busy road, with me running behind him, pushing Pearl in the pram, and yelling at him to stop.

That night when my terror had abated, I sat James down and had a serious discussion. "You are never ever to go on the back of a bike again." I told him sternly. "I know Chinese people do it all the time, but that is not what we do in Australia and certainly not what we do in our family."

James's protests fell on deaf ears, for I was not to be moved from my position.

That weekend was Mother's Day and in Sunday school the children made special cards for us.

James wrote a special message in the card to me:

Sorrey Mum. but I do not want to be in your familee any moor.

I didn't know whether to be proud of his amazing writing skills at only five years of age or sad that he didn't want to be in our family, but I knew that day that he would much rather have a cool Chinese Mum who took him to school each day on the back of a bike than an overly cautious Western one who nagged about road safety and wouldn't even let him buy his own fireworks!

Some days the cultural differences were stressful enough that all of us yearned to catch the next plane home. On those days I would stand in the courtyard and as soon as I heard an overhead plane on its way to Hong Kong or Beijing, I looked up immediately to catch a glimpse of it just before it went through the layer of pollution. It gave me hope that going home was still a possibility. One day.

One sunny Saturday morning in spring was particularly stressful. We lived in a large apartment block, as most people in Chinese cities do. At least two thousand people shared our playground, which consisted of two swings and a few pieces of exercise equipment.

Thomas and his friends loved to ride their skateboards and bikes, play hide-and-seek and soccer in this area. The weekend had started well, with the boys eagerly eating breakfast and then heading outside to play. But this day the play stopped abruptly when a white-faced, crying Thomas appeared at our door. It turns out that he had been dragged along by the hood of his jacket and hit on the face by the lady who cared for the grounds. His crime? He had run across the grass. Something you do every day in Australia but is against the rules in China. It was a hard lesson for us all to learn, and this rule took poor Thomas a while to get used to. I think it may have taken the caretaker a while to recover too, as she was faced with an irate Australian Mum yelling at her in a mixture of Chinese, English, and sign language.

We gradually learnt about other unwritten rules. Whilst pushing in queues, spitting, and urinating on the pavement were okay, water pistols, paper airplanes, and playing soccer in parks were not.

We were also constantly badgered by our lack of child care when we let our children outside without wearing the twenty layers of clothing prescribed by the local grannies. It was funny and kind of nice for about a week, but the joy turned to frustration as I realized that we could not venture outside without attracting a lot of attention.

I had just discovered another 'honeymoon period'—Chinese language learning. I was beginning to understand what people were saying, which was not always a good thing.

"Look at that foreign mother who doesn't put enough clothes on her children."

"Are you cold?"

"You know that if you get cold you will get sick."

These are just a few of the statements I would hear far too frequently. They were usually accompanied by the concerned women pinching the boys' cheeks and feeling the thickness of their clothing, all the while giving me disapproving looks.

The boys initially thought it was funny and would intentionally go outside without jackets, scarves, gloves, and ear warmers; however, I did not enjoy the extra attention or that because so many women stopping me to scold me, it took me twenty minutes to walk what should take me only ten minutes.

It was impossible to pretend that the boys weren't my children, because we were the only people without black hair in the community. We certainly couldn't get "lost in the crowd." I decided the only way to make light of the situation was to charge the boys one yuan every time someone commented on their lack of appropriate attire. The first day I instituted this moneymaking scheme, I earned fifteen yuan from each child in a ten-minute walk!

James sulked and said, "I'm not playing this game anymore."

He did, however, wear his jacket the next time we went out.

A minor victory.

Sometimes the cultural differences amazed and astounded me. The more I learnt to speak Chinese, the more I learnt about how different our Australian culture is from the Chinese.

Chatting to taxi drivers was often interesting, and they were keen to hear all about Australia and our culture. Within minutes of learning that I was Australian and not American, they would ask me all about kangaroos, our work, and lifestyle.

"Do you eat kangaroos?"

"What about koalas?"

"I hear that there are more people in Shanghai than the whole of Australia."

"Are all Australians good swimmers?" (Often asked around the time of the Olympic games.)

And my personal favourite: "Does your country know you have so many kids? Is it okay with them?" Many a taxi driver was amazed and even jealous that we were "allowed" to have more than one child!

One day the kids and I caught a taxi in the centre of town, about a thirty-minute drive to our home in a city of nine million. Before I even told him our address, he said, "I know you. I took you to an apartment in the south of the city a year ago." He then proceeded to tell me the exact address of our apartment.

I was flabbergasted that in a city packed with people and often teeming with tourists, he had remembered me. I was even more shocked with what he said next. "You had this tiny baby with you. Too thin." He shook his head disapprovingly.

"This is her." I excitedly said, pointing to a chubby Pearl with pink cheeks and hair clips in her rapidly growing hair.

He was so shocked and stared at her so hard in the rearview mirror that we almost veered into incoming traffic.

Even in a city this big, I couldn't be camouflaged. I realized that in shops, taxis, and on buses, my actions as a foreigner and a Christian were being noticed and remembered.

Julie Mallinson

"People are watching the way we act, more than they are listening to what we say."

—Max Lucado

My friends and I often joked that we had many TMC days—Too Much China. On these days, I wondered what I was doing in China. The familiar doubts would revisit: Is this really what God wanted for us? All this hardship and we aren't even doing anything.

I really expected that all the hassle would have amazing benefits. I felt sure that the 'real missionaries' endured hardships, but I bet they changed lives and communities too. Didn't they?

One TMC day occurred while on our way to church. To get there we had a ninety-minute bus ride, when we'd have to stand and balance ourselves on a tiny hot bus the whole way. By the time we arrived at church for the two-hour service, our kids were already tired, hot, and hungry.

On this particular day, we lined up to catch the bus. I pulled out my crumpled one-yuan note to buy the boys an 'oil stick', literally a stick of batter deep-fried in oil—the closest thing to doughnuts in China. Being a naive Westerner, I politely waited my turn as person after person pushed ahead of me, leant over me, paid their money, and walked off with their deep-fried delight.

Before I could get the oil sticks, I saw the bus rounding the corner and dragged the protesting boys onto it without their precious breakfast. As I stood on the bus, craning to look out the window, once again I began to feel sorry for myself and wonder if we were actually doing anything useful in China.

We arrived at church tired and disgruntled. I looked around at the other people, a collection of teachers, language students, evangelists, and business people. They all looked happy and at peace with life in China. Certainly they weren't the type of people to want to give it all up over a piece of deep-fried dough.

Only years later did I read and appreciate this quote by Steven Furtick I found on his Twitter page (@stevenfurtick, May 10, 2011): "The reason we struggle with insecurity is because we compare our behind the scenes with everyone else's highlight reel."

On that Sunday morning, the wisdom of that quote eluded me as I sat with Pearl wriggling on my lap and the boys slumping beside me, still mourning their lack of breakfast.

"Think about what you came to China for," the pastor began. "Was it to serve orphans, evangelize university students, or encourage Chinese church leaders?" the pastor asked this conglomerate of Australians, Nepalese, Americans, and Pakistanis.

"Would you be happy if in a year, ten years, or twenty years from now you returned to your home country and achieved none of those things but grew closer to God? Would that be enough for you? Because it would be enough for Him!"

He went on to speak about God's desire to be close to us and how our main desire should be to grow closer to Him. He shared several verses: 'My soul thirsts for God, for the living God. When can I go and meet with God'? - Psalm 42:2; 'Create in me a pure heart, O God, and renew a steadfast spirit within me. Do not cast me from your presence or take your Holy Spirit from me. Restore to me the joy of your salvation and grant me a willing spirit, to sustain me' - Psalm 51:10–12; 'Come near to God and he will come near to you' James 4:8.

Over the following days, I pondered the truth of the Pastor's words. I knew that through earthquakes and home schooling, seeing orphans and meeting Pearl that I had grown closer to God. I was challenged not to look at what I was achieving in China but at what He was achieving in me.

As Oswald Chambers so wisely said, "If I am devoted to the cause of humanity only, I will soon be exhausted and come to the place where my love will falter; but if I love Jesus Christ personally and passionately, I can serve humanity."

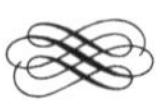

Despite my sincere efforts, more and more cultural differences made me feel like a wai gouren, an 'outsider' as we are called in Chinese. No matter what I did, whether it was my cooking, cleaning, or child care, I seemed to be wrong and the endless criticism wore me down.

Our visa application and even the airport signs described us as 'aliens', and that is certainly how I felt. I had landed on another planet where I was made to feel incapable of caring for my young!

A good friend and I had begun praying together every Saturday morning in McDonald's—a funny place to pray in Australia, but even stranger in a country known for its persecution of Christians. Armed with a hash brown and sausage McMuffin, along with the knowledge that no one could understand us, we discussed our week, the highs and lows, paint that was falling off the walls, foster children we couldn't adopt, and grannies telling us what bad parents we were.

One day she shared her favourite verse of the week, which reminded me once again that God was looking after all of us. 'He defends the cause of the fatherless and the widow, and loves the alien, giving him food and clothing' (Deuteronomy 10:18).

We were both comforted that He was not only caring for our precious foster children but also for us as we lived as aliens in a foreign land.

Chapter Twelve

Living with a Leper

It became apparent to our family and friends in Australia that we weren't returning anytime soon. So instead they visited us, and we were blessed to have them.

Sam's Dad, my parents, and great friends from our hometown all arrived at the local airport and were subject to our version of China.

We were excited to show them our new lifestyle, taste the food, and experience the markets, but most of all we wanted them to meet Pearl. She loved meeting new people. If she saw that the boys approved of the visitors, she would quickly toddle over to them to be cuddled and kissed, receiving much attention.

It had never crossed her mind that she wasn't one of us. She was truly part of our family now, and it was great for us to see that our extended family and friends welcomed her with open arms—literally. We are fortunate to have such supportive families and friends. We hear all sorts of horror stories about people being disowned and marginalized due to caring for an HIV-positive child. We were surprised to discover that even in the West, as well as in China, much fear and discrimination remains.

Taking in a foster child whilst living as an expat in a foreign country is crazy enough (some would argue that just living in a foreign country is crazy!), but to take in the lowest of the low? Children that even the orphanages didn't want? That was something that many people just couldn't understand! We knew early on that we were risking a lot in having Pearl in our home. If our building superintendent or landlord knew of her status, we would be evicted. We would be unwelcome at local shops and restaurants. We knew that she would never be welcome at school or preschool.

I discovered this the hard way when looking to hire help to care for her and clean the house. Home schooling, caring for Pearl, and occasionally doing medical work was getting harder as she became more mobile. She was quick to push all of James's sight word cards onto the floor and scribble on Thomas's spelling book. Some days it took me half the day just to get through the boys' spelling words with the almost constant interruptions from an inquisitive toddler. If she wasn't interrupting our schooling, she was busily flushing jewelry, makeup, and the boys' toys down the toilet!

I began to look for someone to care part-time for Pearl. I hoped that she could be taken for a walk outside and to play on the swings as I schooled the boys; however, word had already spread through the local Chinese community that Pearl had HIV.

Some people I'd asked to help said a downright no, whilst others said that even though they themselves weren't afraid of HIV, they couldn't touch her because then they would suffer discrimination. One Chinese lady taught Sunday school and knew she would be asked to resign if the church found out that she had touched an HIV-positive child. Despite that she saw me every day in the playground, holding Pearl's hand, pushing her on the swings, and playing with the boys, she was still unwilling to risk her own reputation to be associated with us. Another loved Pearl and had no concerns, but her husband refused to let her work for us for fear that she would contract the virus and give it to their children.

Discouragement settled on me as I could find no one to help me care for her. I resigned myself to find someone just to help around the house with washing the dishes, mopping the floors, and such. I figured that even this would give me more time. I could care for Pearl, and the helper could just do chores around the house without having to touch

Pearl. Instead of doing my housecleaning while Pearl took her two-hour midday sleep, I could get two hours solid school work done.

When I discovered that the cleaning woman employed by our Christian company to help the foreigners wouldn't enter our house because of Pearl, I was completely disheartened. That she wouldn't even walk through our front door broke my heart!

When my friend broke this news to me, I surprised her by bursting into tears. No, I wasn't crying because I would have to mop my own floors, but for Pearl and all the other children like her throughout China. Pearl was such a loving, kind little girl who needed to be touched and cuddled. And she had no idea that people couldn't stand to be near her.

As a mother is hurt when her child is bullied and teased at school, I was hurt by the discrimination Pearl was suffering. Because we were harboring an 'untouchable', I felt the isolation and vulnerability of a leper.

"The problem isn't with the ones that hide in shame; it's with the ones that shame them into hiding," say Carolyn and Kiel Twietmyer, adoptive parents of Selah Twietmyer, an HIV/AIDS-infected teen (http://youtu.be/sRxDRzZxDbI).

It was only much later, thanks to our wonderful friends at Project Hopeful that I realized the problem wasn't with us or Pearl, an innocent child who just happened to have a 'bug in her blood', but with those who were unwilling to reach out and touch the lepers of the community as Jesus did. 'Filled with compassion, Jesus reached out his hand and touched the man. '*I am willing,' he said. 'Be clean*!'' Mark 1:41.

How I wish I had known these people from Project Hopeful, a group that educates, encourages, and enables families and individuals to adopt children with HIV/AIDS. I needed their support on those dark days in China when we felt so alone as we battled the misconceptions and fear that surrounded us and Pearl.

When I heard the news that our cleaner wouldn't even enter our house, I vowed never to leave Pearl in China. For her to be adopted into another family in another country would have broken my heart. But for her to stay in China would have broken her heart and spirit and ruin her life forever.

> *'Your compassion is great, O LORD; preserve my life according to your laws. Many are the foes who persecute me.'*
>
> —Psalm 119:156–157

Gradually we were able to leave our scarves, gloves, hats, and coats at home as the weather warmed and we approached the summer of 2009. We had agreed to manage a 'Bring Me Hope' summer camp in Xian. We strongly believed that this was a great way to help orphans and impact foreigners regarding the plight of the orphan. So we busily booked hotels, found staff, ordered meals, and found a swimming pool that wasn't too green with algae.

We were to host four weeks of camp in a three-star hotel in the centre of our city. Every week we would meet different children, translators, and volunteers and enjoy a schedule packed with craft, sports, swimming, and special times in the family unit.

This was our third camp, and we knew that amongst the happiness there was much heartache as these children who had finally found love had to return to the lonely life in an orphanage after just five short days. It all seemed too short and too hard.

As I watched kids blossom, laugh, and cuddle with their volunteers, all I could think of was how hard the good-bye day would be. Deep down I knew that camp was a great thing. Studies show that children who have formed a bond and felt love sometime in their lives will be able to bond and cope better later in life. Even if that love lasted only five days, it was five days that the child would always remember and treasure, and five days that would build their self-esteem. They could say that sometime, somewhere they had been loved.

Our first week was particularly hard. We had a disabled and traumatized sixteen-year-old I'll call Fiona (not her real name), who was violent and threatening. This poor girl was aggressive to everyone and unwilling to be touched or loved. She had lived in a particularly difficult orphanage for many years and was unwilling to trust anyone. Every day we struggled to control her as she threatened staff by wielding rubbish bins. More than once she was taken kicking and screaming from the dining room after attacking another child.

One night as we prayed about her and surveyed the damage she had inflicted that day, James, then seven, asked innocently, "If we didn't take Pearl, she would be like that too, wouldn't she?"

It was hard to imagine that Pearl, who was all sweetness and light and loved by everyone, could end up this way. I knew, however, that it certainly was a possibility if she lived a life of abandonment, abuse, and isolation. James's wise comment reminded me that I needed to understand what these children had experienced and not just be annoyed at them for disrupting camp.

On the third day of week one, our bus ran into the hotel! (We are still unsure how a bus can run into a hotel.) We were busy trying to manage the usual adjustment problems with staff, translator, and volunteer relationships. We also had one little boy of ten who made things particularly challenging and heartbreaking.

'Jo' had attended the camp in another city the year before. A few weeks after that camp he ran away from the orphanage and walked for three days back to the campsite. He must have been disappointed to discover that it was by then deserted. He was eventually found and taken back to the orphanage despite his protests.

A year later he was now entering his second camp, with a swagger and a knowing smile. He knew all about the swimming, ball games, great food, and the love he would receive—and he was back for more! This year started as usual, with a huge Chinese banquet. This was always a crazy time as we sat together and shared a great array of Chinese dishes. Most of the foreign volunteers were gingerly trying chopsticks for the first time, and most of the children were delighted to see such a selection of food after a bland diet of rice, noodles, and vegetables served in the orphanage. Inevitably some children would eat so much they would vomit. They had never had access to so much delicious food and, hence, would eat as quickly as they could, shoveling the food into their mouths and barely chewing. Add to this Fiona and the high level of excitement felt by all the children as they took in their new surroundings, and the meal time was a busy one. In fact, it was a recipe for disaster!

This year was no exception, and once I had finished disaster control in one area, I looked around to see Jo sitting forlornly at a table by himself. What I later discovered was that the Chinese translators had discovered that Jo had Hepatitis B. They banished him from their table and forced him to eat alone. There he sat at a table set for ten. An outcast! The smile had vanished from his face as he watched his friends laughing and playing in their family groups, yet he, like a leper, was isolated and abandoned. Again!

I lost any semblance of love, peace, tolerance, and self-control as I tried to explain to these university students the truth about Hepatitis B. Even though up to 10 percent of the people in China are carriers of the Hepatitis B virus and it is not transmitted by chopsticks, it was still common to treat people like this, to turn their backs on them and isolate them. Orphans particularly were shunned from the community. They had no parents or family to defend them.

Heaven help us all if people knew of Pearl's condition.

Mother Teresa knew well the plight of the outcasts like Jo. She said, "Loneliness and the feeling of being unwanted is the most terrible poverty."

The last night of camp was a particularly difficult night as the kids who had been to camp before knew that the good-bye day was fast approaching. Despite the laughter at the talent show, a somber mood descended that night as the new (and only) 'families' settled their kids into bed for the last time. As the children were being read their final good-night stories, we discovered that Jo was missing. He had climbed out his window and was threatening to jump from his third-floor bedroom. He said that if he broke his leg, he would be able to stay in our city and not have to return to his orphanage the following day.

With much coaxing and prayer we finally drew him back into his room and tucked him into bed, but the experience left us all wondering: How hard is his life in the orphanage that he would rather be in a Chinese hospital with a broken leg?

Over the next three weeks of camp, we had one more orphan threaten the window jump, and fortunately the bus managed to stay clear of hitting the hotel again.

But the toll of four good-bye days was adding up. I began to wonder about the futility of our time in China. Were we helping anyone? How could we mend the broken hearts of these children? They obviously needed so much more than medical care. They needed love, games, education, affection, and so much more.

I began to think and pray about what my role would be, and a very small seed was planted in my mind. After seeing the treatment Jo received at the dinner table, I more and more realized how hard life was for Hepatitis B and HIV-positive children, the so-called 'contagious children.'

How could I help them? Could we possibly give more of them the hope and love that Pearl had blossomed under? Max Lucado wrote, "No one can do everything, but everyone can do something." What was the something I could do?

On the very last night of camp one of our orphans touched all of us. I had to write in my journal that night about it.

'The end of our week-long orphan camp arrived. Once again we had a great week of crafts, swimming, singing, and building lifelong friendships.

On the final night we all sat and readied ourselves for our end-of-week talent quest and concert, something taken very seriously by the children as they all sang, danced, and acted to the admiration of staff, volunteers, and translators.

One boy whom we loved asked to sing a song.

Sixteen-year-old Albert, a boy with severe cerebral palsy, couldn't walk, talk, or eat without difficulty, yet he was extremely clever.

He had been abandoned by his parents at eight years of age, when the pressures of physical care became too much for them. There are no wheelchair ramps, disabled access, or even child-sized wheelchairs in China.

We expected a Chinese version of 'heads, shoulders, knees, and toes' or the 'Hokey Pokey', but this sixteen-year-old chose to thank God for the great week he had a camp.

He sang 'Give Thanks with a Grateful Heart', a song well-known to most of us and taught to him by Christians caring for him in the orphanage.

We stood in awe as he sang, 'And now let the weak say I am strong, let the poor say I am rich because of what the Lord has done for me.'

A sixteen-year-old, wheelchair-bound, recently abandoned orphan singing to us about the weak and the poor. It was one of those China moments when I realized that I came here to help them, but more often than not they help me.'

Camp was over for another year. As foreigners boarded planes for the United States, Canada, and Australia, translators travelled on overnight trains to their hometowns, and the children went back to daily life in an orphanage, our family packed up the life jackets, craft supplies, and lice shampoo and returned home.

In a year so much had changed in our lives that I couldn't help but wonder what we would be doing at the conclusion of camp in a year's time.

Thomas no longer cried every night for lack of friends as he ran off to play with the many neighborhood children eagerly awaiting his return.

James continued to amaze us with his reading and writing skills, but also his compassion and love for others.

Instead of watching the Tupperware family out our window, we had our very own 'recycled' child who had miraculously been recycled from death's door to energetic toddler.

> *'Be joyful always; pray continually; give thanks in all circumstances, for this is God's will for you in Christ Jesus.'*
>
> —1 Thessalonians 5:16–18

Chapter Thirteen

Pauper to Princess

Not long after camp we again were blessed to have visitors. Autumn, although brief, was a great time to visit Xian to avoid the scorching summers and freezing winters that we experienced in central China. Most Aussies could cope with the summers, but few visitors were keen to leave the sun, surf, and sand of an Australian summer for the below-zero temperatures of a Chinese winter.

Sam's parents arrived in September and we were all excited to see them and receive the gifts they bought. The boys loved playing with toys sent over by their cousins, and Pearl was delighted with the pink Barbie dress she received from her Aussie aunty. Much twirling, dancing and self-admiration ensued.

After showing them the sights of Xian, we decided to head south to the town of Pearl's orphanage. We were excited to introduce them to some of the children we had grown to know and love at camp and also try to visit the group home that Pearl lived in for the four months before we took her in. So amidst the confused stares from the locals, six foreigners and one little Chinese girl boarded the bus for Hanzhong. Always a beautiful trip through the mountains, this time proved no exception. We left the pollution of Xian and ascended the clear mountains shrouded in brilliant autumn colors.

The boys loved counting the tunnels between Xian and Hanzhong. Unlike the windy mountain roads in Australia, the Chinese engineers had managed to tunnel through the Qing Ling mountain range, resulting in a total of over seventy tunnels on the four-hour journey.

The boys munched happily on their snacks as they counted the tunnels and admired the scenery: trees, mountains, crystal clear rivers, and even blue sky. All amazing parts of God's creation we hadn't seen in months.

Every time we sped over these mountains the scenery was different. Snow-covered mountain peaks and frozen streams, amazing autumn colors and rice paddies filled with shimmering water, and the swaying green fronds of rice plants. It was so refreshing for our family to escape the city and see the splendour of God's world once again. We were reminded of the beauty of creation and not to take it for granted. As Max Lucado said more eloquently than I ever could: "Nature is God's first missionary. Where there is no Bible there are sparkling stars. Where there are not preachers there are spring times. If a person has nothing but nature, then nature is enough to reveal something about God."

Pearl sat happily on my lap, listening to my iPod, playing with her dolls, and sipping water from her new Barbie drink bottle. I thought back to her last trip over these mountains. A foreign volunteer had brought the frail, listless child with end-stage AIDS over these very mountains in the hope of getting some medical treatment. Now here she was returning to her hometown. A bundle of energy, sporting pigtails, and an inquisitive personality, she was blissfully unaware of how unwell she had been the last time she traversed this very road.

After arriving in Hanzhong, we settled into our two-star hotel room and rested before a hectic day at the orphanage.

It had taken us a while to get accustomed to most Chinese hotels having only twin rooms. Despite inquiring many times for a family room and pointing emphatically at the children, the hotel staff would look at us with blank stares and give us a key to yet another twin room. Finally it dawned on us that in China, most families only have one child, who shares a bed with Mum. The thought of sharing a hard, single bed with any of my children didn't appeal to me, so we learnt to book two twin rooms in advance to ensure a decent night's sleep for us all.

For old time's sake, we treated Sam's parents to a delicious meal of fried chicken at KFC and then returned to the hotel.

The next day we rose bright and early, and after a typical hotel breakfast of boiled egg, rice porridge, and pickled vegetables we headed off to the orphanage about ten minutes out of town. The orphanage Pearl came from consisted of a number of group homes. Each home had a house mama who was responsible for the care of up to eight children. They worked twenty-fours hours a day with one weekend off a month and were paid less than AU$100 a month.

A number of children with differing special needs lived in each home. Their special needs included severe cerebral palsy, spina bifida, and blindness or deafness. Most babies were looked after in a nursery, but because of her HIV, Pearl had not been accepted at the nursery and was instead sent to a busy group home.

I can't begin to imagine how hectic life must be for the group home mamas. When Sam was away, I struggled being a Mum to three healthy children. But to be a single Mum to eight children, some needing specialized feeding, some wheelchair bound, and some with severe illnesses seemed to me an impossible task.

I couldn't remember much about Pearl's mama except that she told us how tired she was with caring for seven kids during the day and having to be up all night with Pearl crying, coughing, and vomiting! I hoped we could meet her again and thank her for being the only caregiver in that orphanage willing to risk caring for Pearl. If not for her, we probably wouldn't have Pearl as part of our family.

First, we visited the children from camp. We saw sixteen-year-old Albert, who had loved every minute of camp and delighted us all with singing a wonderful praise song on the last day. Once again, he enjoyed singing to us and proudly showed us his presents from camp and the 'memory book' he'd made, which was prominently displayed in a safe place in the bedroom he shared with three other boys. A few other children recognised us and ran up, eagerly showing us their camp

T-shirts and craft projects. With hope shining in their eyes, they said, "Next summer? We go to big hotel again? We go swimming?" How could we refuse?

We reluctantly left them to find the home where we first met Pearl on a hot summer day a year ago. I vaguely remembered its location and looked around for some caregivers that might remember her. Because it was a weekend, no English-speaking staff was available, so we had to rely on our Chinese. Sadly, my Chinese skills hadn't improved much since the birthday cake fiasco.

Eventually I recognized a couple of caregivers whom I had met when Pearl was there. They were a married couple who had cared for her occasionally, and I had spent an hour reassuring them that they hadn't caught HIV from applying cream to Pearl's dry, cracked feet. I nervously approached them and announced to them that Pearl was visiting and pointed to her. She was a chubby little girl by then and was running around the playground, completely oblivious to what was happening.

The caregivers looked at me as if I had gone crazy as I continued to repeat her name. I am not sure if I got the tones right. I could have been saying 'government house dog' for all I knew. Finally, I explained how they had a little girl who was very sick with HIV a few years ago. I thought I'd gotten the message across.

They shook their heads sadly. "She went to Xian and died."

"No, no. That is her." I pointed to the chubby girl in the Esprit dress going down the slide.

I could understand their disbelief. Nothing would budge their conviction that the happy, healthy-looking girl on the slide was a different child, not the wasted rag doll they had sent to the hospital a year ago. I was about to abandon my quest when suddenly I remembered Sam's phone. His phone contained countless photos of Pearl when we had first met her and cared for her in the hospital. He had captured many photos of the depressed, wasted orphan, following her miraculous change that occurred over the following few months.

So we seized the phone and nervously scrolled through the hundreds of photos to find those initial photos of Pearl, a despondent, dejected little girl barely making a bump on a hospital bed. We showed the couple the phone and suddenly there were shrieks of excitement as they called out her Chinese name (pronounced correctly). They called out to anyone who would listen, and soon we were surrounded by many bleary-eyed staff who had awoken from their midday sleep.

"She is here. She is here!" they yelled as Pearl ran around their feet.

"Where?" her former mama asked, looking eagerly around the playground. She looked right past the chubby toddler at her feet and certainly didn't recognize her as the terminally ill child she had cared for a year ago. Disbelief and then amazement shone in her eyes when we explained to her that this indeed was Pearl.

She immediately lifted her up and cuddled her, talking loudly and quickly in Chinese, much to the consternation of poor Pearl, who was left wondering who this Chinese woman was who referred to herself as Mama.

The caregivers passed her from one to another, pinching her plump arms and exclaiming in delight. There is only one thing better than a child in many layers of clothing, and that is a chubby child. They gave me looks of approval that I had managed to help her gain weight so well. Little did they know that it was not me but the medicine and people all over the world praying for her. Maybe the odd bowl of dumplings had helped too!

It was an emotional and overwhelming time, which Sam's Dad managed to capture on video. Many excited Chinese voices all talked at once and I tried to understand them. Pearl stood in their midst, like a royal princess enjoying all the attention but wondering what it was all about. In an orphanage where she had been destined for a storage shed because no one was willing to care for her, she had now reached celebrity status. Not only was she touched, but she was hugged, kissed, and given food parcels. Her house mama ran into the group home and came out with a tattered photo of Pearl in a pram surrounded by the other children. She eagerly pressed it into my hand to keep as a souvenir, as she gave a bemused Pearl a banana with the other.

So with banana and photos, memories of Albert, and a great deal of video footage, courtesy of Sam's Dad and his new video camera, we squeezed into a taxi and left the orphanage. As our taxi pulled away, caregivers and children pressed their faces to the glass and energetically waved good-bye and invited us to 'Come back soon.'

Despite the taxi being so crowded so that we were sitting on one another's laps, it was a farewell fit for royalty. It wasn't until we returned to the hotel that night and devoured even more fried chicken that I realized that they had all touched her! No amount of pamphlets, education sessions, videos, or news reports would replace the education session we had just given. A child who had literally come back to life and now had a hope and future in their very midst had convinced them that HIV wasn't the dreaded death sentence they had assumed.

> *'But God chose the foolish things of the world to shame the wise; God chose the weak things of the world to shame the strong.'*
>
> —1 Corinthians 1:27

I prayed that this would change their hearts and minds so that any future HIV-positive children who came to them would receive better treatment and understanding.

Over the next few months we took life a day at a time.

We applied to take Pearl back to Australia on a medical visa for a few weeks. We waited hopefully for a reply, as we were all desperate to return home for a break. It had now been over eighteen months since we'd left Australia for a 'one year' volunteer post in China.

Many days we would get caught up in the cycle of school work, cooking, and shopping. The boys and I were miraculously surviving home schooling, and I think, although they refused to admit it, that they were even learning something! They loved playing with local friends.

It turned out that Americans, Koreans, and even Chinese boys are all pretty much the same. They played together happily for hours with skateboards, cartoon figures, sticks and balls, and there was rarely a night when we didn't have someone to join us for a sleepover or at least for dinner.

Some days we wouldn't see Thomas and James for hours as they played with friends outside. I never begrudged them the time with friends, as I remembered so well our early days in China when Thomas cried every night because he had no friends.

I was amused, though, at how our lives had changed.

Whilst living in Australia just two years prior, Thomas would often return home from friends' homes, terribly jealous. "Luke has the best pool," or "Daniel has an Xbox," or "Jo has a pool and a trampoline," and even once to my dismay, "Paul has a better water view than we do." The list would go on.

One day whilst living in China, he returned home from his American friends' house. "Ike has the best house," he started, and I braced myself for what amazing toy Ike had that we didn't own (and probably never would). "When someone takes a shower, the toilet doesn't get wet and they don't even have to mop the floor."

Sam and I laughed so much that we had gone from comparing water views to showers and toilets!

Pearl was growing up fast and was amazing us all with her English language skills that merged with a few important Chinese words. Her hair had survived the shaving in the orphanage and was growing just long enough for pigtails. She loved her many pink and purple hair clips, pink silk pajamas, and, of course, fairy dresses, wings, and wands. She had reached the magical TV age and was happy to watch DVDs whilst I home schooled the boys.

Her favourite pastime was to dress up as a princess, complete with my high-heeled shoes, and dance around the lounge room, admiring herself in the reflection in the windows. We started calling her 'princess', which suited her perfectly. "The princess is hungry," or "The princess needs to go to bed," or "The princess wants to watch TV" were statements that were heard far too often as Sam, the boys, and I ran around, making her life happy and comfortable. Subconsciously we thought that spoiling her would make up for the past hurts in her short life.

So, the days were mostly filled with fun and happiness as we watched our children grow up and gradually become accustomed to life in China. It wasn't until nighttime that I would worry. I often sat up late at night with a cup of hot chocolate, writing my thoughts and feelings to give myself some clarity and perspective.

September 2009

It is nearly midnight on an unusually cold September night in China. I write because I am unable to sleep, and I am tormented by fears, worries, and even sadness.

I write not knowing how this story will end, but knowing that all I can do now is to trust in God and His promises and trust that He is in control. Even though I don't know what the future holds for our family, I know that He does.

I recently read a quote by H.E Manning that challenged my way of thinking and coping with the unknown:

"Neither go back in fear and misgiving to the past nor in anxiety and forecasting to the future, but lie quiet under His hand, having no will but his."

As are all good things, it is so much easier said than done, but as I sit in the still of the night, I pray that God gives me the strength to live in the moment. Not the past or future.

As I write, a little girl sleeps soundly in our three-bedroom apartment in central China. She is dressed in her favourite pink pajamas and covered by her pink blanket decorated with a multitude of flowers. After being sung her favourite song, 'Jesus Loves Me', her last words tonight were, "I love you, Mama."

Her name is Pearl, and a year ago she was found on the roadside outside an Internet cafe. She has HIV and was abandoned at fifteen months, probably by a family member who loved her but could no longer cope with her illness.

This is her story but has now become ours as we love her as our own daughter.

On sleepless nights like tonight I can only pray and trust that 'His ways are higher than our ways' and pray that the God who has lifted this girl from the dust heap can help me sleep in peace. I pray that she can be taken from a life of sadness and neglect to the life of a princess that she deserves.

> *'I will lie down and sleep in peace, for you alone, O* Lord, *make me dwell in safety.'*
>
> —Psalm 4:8

> *However, as it is written: 'No eye has seen, no ear has heard, no mind has conceived what God has prepared for those who love him.'*
>
> —1 Corinthians 2:9

Chapter Fourteen

The Glad Game

As our visitors left and the winter season drew nearer, depression became an unwanted companion. I was sick of living in China. I was desperate to return home to friends, family, and the Australian sunshine. But we couldn't travel with Pearl.

Our medical visas had been denied, which was not surprising yet still disappointing. So we were destined to spend another cold winter and Christmas in China. The thought of leaving her was too hard to bear. We wouldn't enjoy Christmas in Australia without the newest member of our family.

Friends sent me Christmas photos showing them sipping cocktails on the beach; I looked outside at the frozen spit on the pavement and the grey landscape. I was so desperate for even a bit of home that I got excited when I saw green in the distance! Looking harder to determine what could be this bubble of color in a backdrop of muted neutrals, I realized it was scaffolding on a building site!

Many foreigners managed to go home for the Christmas season, deepening my sense of isolation. Feeling very sorry for myself and trapped in China, I felt like this was my forty years in the wilderness. It may be hard to believe, but I was doing a lot more complaining than the Israelites did!

However, a few events occurred that made me realize how lucky I was. So I willed myself to try to count my blessings. Sometimes it is easy for me to look at what I want that others have rather than appreciate the many precious things I have. God sent people and events into my life to show me how fortunate I really was.

One day I was talking to a friend about her ayi, the woman who helped care for her children and cooked their meals. Most of these workers lived in the villages and came into cities to work for foreigners.

My friend had been asking her to cook with eggs or meat at least three times a week so that the children would have protein. Many Chinese people, especially the poorer villagers, eat just rice and whatever vegetables are in the garden. Eggs and meat are expensive and rarely used and only for special occasions.

The ayi complied and thought that it was such a great idea, she determined to do the same for her children. On the following weekend she walked to the next village to buy eggs. Eggs don't come in cartons in China, so she carefully placed them in her shopping bag. When she arrived home, she was disappointed to discover that all but one of her precious eggs had broken in the plastic bag! How sad not to be able to provide your own children with the basic necessities of life.

We Westerners worry so much about our children. Should they be doing soccer, ballet, or music lessons—or all three? Is it fair that they are the only kids on their class without a pool? (My children think it's not fair.) How are they doing in school? Should they have extra tuition?

But I never had to worry that I couldn't afford to give my kids meat or buy them clothing for winter. As I cooked the kids their favourite meal, lasagna, I began to understand how lucky I was that I didn't have to struggle financially to meet my kids' basic needs.

A few weeks after this revelation, I visited an amazing foster family. This poor family who lived in a village had two children of their own and fostered three children with severe cerebral palsy. All three foster children were unable to eat, speak, or even toilet themselves. So this man and his humble wife managed to care for five children in a two-bedroom house with no heat or running water.

He proudly showed me outside where he had fashioned a toilet out of a broken chair and old rags. He could tell when his foster children needed to go the toilet by grimaces on their faces or beads of sweat on their foreheads. He would then take them outside to the sub-zero temperatures to the toilet, which was far better than using the public toilets like most other villagers did. My Chinese teacher had recently told me that 75 percent of houses in China don't have a toilet. Residents share public bathrooms. I needed to stop complaining about my tiny, smelly Chinese bathroom and start appreciating that I even had one!

After we got home from visiting this family, I cranked up the heat, took a long hot shower, put on my warmest clothes, drank multiple cups of hot chocolate, but I still could not stop shivering from getting chilled while in that family's cold house.

Whenever people say, "You guys are amazing fostering and loving Pearl," I think of this man and his wife. They had taken on three disabled children and thus were scorned by neighbors. They had no heat, toilet, new clothes, nor did they receive any Christmas gift packs. Months later I discovered a verse that described this family perfectly:

> *'Out of the most severe trial, their overflowing joy and their extreme poverty welled up in rich generosity. For I testify that they gave as much as they were able, and even beyond their ability. Entirely on their own, they urgently pleaded with us for the privilege of sharing in this service to the saints.'*
>
> —2 Corinthians 8:2–4

Their plight affected me, so I told friends at the local international school where he worked as a janitor part-time about their situation. I was thrilled when a few months later they organized a fund-raiser for him. With the money received he was able to purchase a hot water heater so they could have running hot water!

Even though I continued to complain about my plight, I must admit that I gradually learnt to look at the many people who had less than me rather than the few people who had more. This is a lesson I repeat to myself and my children almost daily. It is even harder in our comfortable Western countries where we rarely encounter people who have such real and desperate needs.

I never thought that things we took for granted, such as egg cartons and toilets, would be something that I would one day be thankful for.

> *'I am not saying this because I am in need, for I have learned to be content whatever the circumstances.*
>
> *I know what it is to be in need, and I know what it is to have plenty.*

I have learned the secret of being content in any and every situation, whether well fed or hungry, whether living in plenty or in want.'

—Philippians 4:11–12

Just before Christmas we decided to attend the ceremony to mark the twentieth anniversary of Pearl's orphanage. None of us really wanted to attend a Chinese ceremony in the heart of winter, but we thought it would be a good way to meet orphanage directors, in particular her orphanage director, so we could develop favour with her to help us through the ensuing adoption process.

So once again we traversed those mountains, this time blanketed in snow. An icy wind was blowing when we arrived at the orphanage where the ceremony would take place. Hundreds of people milled around outside, chatting and sipping on hot water in paper cups. We and the other foreigners felt conspicuous, as usual, amongst the sea of Chinese faces. Finally an important official ushered us foreigners into a 'waiting room.'

Looking around, we realized that we were in the equivalent of the 'business' class waiting room while the 'economy' class was outside, stamping their feet and blowing on their hands in an attempt to survive the cold. Our foreign status afforded us special treatment.

We sat at a long mahogany carved table. The hosts offered us cups of tea and gave us plates full of peanuts, sunflower seeds, and Chinese candy to munch on. With us sat orphanage directors, government officials, and heads of government civil affairs.

Once the celebration began, we were ushered to the front row of the auditorium for two hours of entertainment, including indoor fireworks, karaoke displays, and many, many speeches, all in Chinese, of course. Both Sam and I marveled that we, and in particular Pearl, had been given such special treatment. The most unloved and unwanted child at the whole orphanage sat at a table with dignitaries—the princes of their people.

'Who is like the Lord *our God, the One who sits enthroned on high, who stoops down to look on the heavens and the earth? He raises the poor from the dust and lifts the needy from the ash heap; he seats them with princes, with the princes of their people.'*

—Psalm 113:5–8

To me it was yet another reminder that instead of complaining, I should be praising God.

Despite my resolution to be cheerful and positive, our friends continued to leave for their home countries and the dreary weather grew drearier as Xian experienced one of its coldest winters. On one of those grey winter days I made another entry in my journal.

January

"It has been a hard weekend. I have spent the weekend in bed with a cold, gradually feeling more and more sorry for myself.

One by one our friends have left for Chinese New Year, and we feel like we are the only foreigners left in this city of nine million.

I can't help but imagine them on the sunny shores of Australia or Thailand as we stay in China and single-handedly battle the fireworks and cold grey skies.

I halfheartedly drag myself out of bed and prepare myself and the boys for another day of 'St. Vidlers Christian College' as we affectionately call our home schooling programme.

I am not sure who is less enthusiastic, me or them.

As usual we start off with a Bible verse from our daily devotional book. The verse for the day is Philippians 4:11: '*For I have learned to be content whatever the circumstances.*'

We talk briefly about contentment before getting on to the dreaded spelling and maths.

It is not until lunch time that I realize the full meaning of the verse.

I have taken to making the boys tomato soup for lunch. They love it so much and tell me it is just as good as the tinned soup in Australia.

(I think that is a compliment.) James even goes as far as to ask if I can make tinned spaghetti too!

So I leave the boys happily playing the Wii and bundle up to brave the snow to buy the 2 kilos of tomatoes I need for my next batch of soup.

The 'veggie man' stands in the snow, his produce on display on the back of his bike. He occasionally brushes the snow off the potatoes, carrots, and tomatoes with his bare hands. His three young children are at home today, but I know they don't have heat and possess barely enough clothes. Often I see them sitting in an old pram with cardboard boxes around then to protect them from the biting winds and snow.

As he counts out the tomatoes, his hands shock me. They are cracked, calloused, and bleeding due to the constant exposure to the cold. In all my years of medicine I have never seen anything like it.

I pass over the eight yuan (AU$1.50) for 2 kilos of tomatoes. He is so happy with such a big sale that he gives me a bunch of coriander for free! I reflect on how amazingly kind he is to give me a discount without a hint of bitterness or jealousy in his heart.

As I arrive home, I struggle to find a hook for my coat amongst Pearl's three. My wet, snowy shoes leave a dirty puddle on our white polished tiles. Normally these inconveniences would make me irate, but today instead of seeing my friends on the beach I see the kind face of the veggie man.

If he can be content despite being constantly freezing and unable to provide for his children, then surely I can cope with a muddy puddle!

Instead of constantly complaining, I tried to distract myself with exercise, study, and even housework! Again I noted in my journal:

"It is nearly two years since we arrived in China. I just realized that, no, my clothes aren't shrinking, and, yes, too much Chinese food is bad for you (not to mention the chocolate bar every night). So I have decided to start jogging in order to lose the extra weight.

So like it or not (usually not), I began jogging at 6 AM. Today is my second day and already I know that jogging in a coastal town in Australia is different from jogging in a city of nine million in China.

Instead of seeing dolphins and the ocean, I now see hundreds of cars, bikes, and trucks. Instead of jumping over logs and branches, I now jump over piles of yesterday's rubbish. Instead of smelling the sea and freshly cut grass, I smell the drains, pollution, and garbage.

"This is so unfair," I have been telling people willing enough to listen. "I used to see dolphins every morning. Look what I gave up to come here." Somehow I convinced myself that I had given up more than anyone else.

I don't deserve this. I deserve to be somewhere else," I told myself.

But one day, well into my moaning, a stronger voice spoke to me. "He deserved to be somewhere else."

Jesus left a place even more beautiful than Australia. He left thrones, singing angels, crystal clear rivers, and gold. He left a place where there is no crying or mourning or night. He came to a dusty, dirty desert.

He deserved more. He went from being God to being treated like an animal. He went from being with angels to being despised and rejected by men.

I pray today that I can appreciate more and more, the great sacrifice that He made for me. I pray that daily He reminds me of what He left and what He endured to save me.

> *'Consider him who endured such opposition from sinful men, so that you will not grow weary and lose heart.'*
>
> —Hebrews 12:3

By then, I had learnt to appreciate egg cartons, toilets, a warm house, and the miracle that unfolded in Pearl's life. I could even go for a jog without feeling too sorry for myself! It seemed that more and more, I was seeing how hard life was for so many people. More and more, I was slowly beginning to realize how blessed I really was and how I was being called to help those less fortunate than myself. I had to only look around to see that the majority of the people in this country were far worse off than I was.

A good friend and I travelled back to Hanzhong to perform another medical clinic. An amazing woman, she was a retired nurse and had lived in China for a year longer than we had. We always enjoyed our times together, reminiscing about life in Australia and laughing at our most recent language difficulties—me telling my teacher that I liked shopping without clothes on, and her telling her teacher that she rides a tomato to lessons!

We had only one day in Hanzhong, so we quickly set up and began attending to the thirty children we had to see that day. Most of them suffered from severe and complicated medical issues that Australian general practitioners would never deal with. Instead, a specialist clinic in a teaching hospital in a major city would see these children. But here we were a part-time GP and a retired nurse trying to sort out untreated heart disease, hydrocephalus, and spina bifida!

I felt like Moses and wanted to ask God for someone better equipped for the job. However, I knew that despite my failings, I was probably the best doctor these kids would ever see within China.

Child after child was placed on the examination table, we heard their stories, examined the children, and offered some useful advice. More often than not, there was nothing we could do or say to help these children. Some babies with severe heart failure didn't qualify for a potentially life-saving operation. Others were severely malnourished, as they were unable to feed properly because of a cleft palate. Toddlers diagnosed with autism and those who were developmentally delayed may just have been suffering from lack of bonding, stimulation, and social interaction. We offered as much support and advice as possible in desperately difficult circumstances.

The last child we saw was a six-week-old girl with spina bifida. She, unlike the other children, was found as a newborn with a note pinned to her:

"The doctor said she needs an operation that will cost 40,000 yuan.
We are farmers and don't have that much money.
Please look after our baby girl."

My friend, Bev, and I were saddened to hear such a desperate plea from these poor villagers. We could feel their hearts breaking as they wrote that last sentence. Our day ended on a sad note as our bus pulled away from the depot and we embarked on the journey home. The little we had done was nowhere near enough to help the children or their grieving parents.

Two days later, Bev rang me. Her voice tingled with excitement. She called to tell me that she was going to start foster homes for these little ones. She already had a house and staff and was soon going to collect some of the sickest babies.

Bev now runs two houses, each containing at least ten children, called Dove's Wings. She cares for the lowest of the low, gives them food, medical care, and, most important, love. I feel so privileged to have been there to witness the beginning of her amazing venture. I hope that those parents who must relinquish their children will one day know the comfort that people like Bev are bringing to them.

> *'Can a mother forget the baby at her breast and have no compassion on the child she has borne?*
>
> *Though she may forget, I will not forget you!*
>
> *See, I have engraved you on the palms of my hands; your walls are ever before me.'*
>
> —Isaiah 49:15–16

Chapter Fifteen

R2 and D2

Sam and I continued to think and pray about our future and what we could do in China. We both still felt called to help orphans in need. But how? Visiting orphanages as medical doctors seemed to just touch the surface. With politics, outbreaks of illness, national holidays, and so on, it seemed that we were lucky to visit orphanages once a month. We were able to give no continuity of care and often just saw children who were acutely ill. Once a month we saw children who had coughs, colds, and rashes, yet the children who were malnourished due to heart failure or a cleft lip and palate rarely improved. It was these children who desperately needed help.

Chinese surgeons wouldn't operate on these children until they reached a certain weight, but they were unable to reach that weight due to their physical illnesses. I had seen more than a few die of starvation whilst awaiting surgery. It felt like much of our advice fell in deaf ears. In one way our advice was culturally inappropriate. It was difficult to change cultural beliefs on occasional visits.

We constantly battled the misuse of antibiotics. Antibiotics can be bought over the counter in China, so most people had two or three courses of antibiotics before even seeing a doctor. Most of the children were given a course of antibiotics whenever they had a cough, fever, or sniffle; hence, the emergence of resistant strains of bacteria, in addition to rashes, and other drug-related side effects.

Telling the staff just to give a child fluids to drink and paracetamol for comfort during an infection was as foreign to them as we were. To our frustration, we often found that the children were started on high doses of an inappropriate antibiotic despite our advice. Much of our advice couldn't be followed due to the constraints of the orphanage environment. Often one caregiver would have up to eight babies to look after. They didn't have the forty minutes it took to painstakingly feed a cleft palate baby, nor did they take the time to regularly apply cream to severe eczema.

Some of the advice I gave reflected how naive I was regarding all things Chinese. At one stage I attended to many of the staff in the middle of winter who had severe fungal foot infections. After advising them which cream to use, I explained how to care for their feet, drying them thoroughly after a shower and even using a hair dryer to make sure they were completely dry.

They looked at one another and laughed. It was only months later that I realized these caregivers didn't have bathrooms in their homes, let alone hair dryers. They bathed weekly in the communal showers down the road, after which they quickly donned socks and shoes and walked back home. My friends told me that they would arrive home with flecks of ice in their wet hair. No wonder they had fungal infections!

Sam and I began to think that the only real way we could help was to take babies out of orphanages. If they were in small foster families, there would be time to love them, feed them, and care for them as much as they deserved. After all, we had seen firsthand the miraculous way this had changed Pearl. We began to talk more and more about helping children with HIV, since that was a huge area of need that God had literally put right in front of our noses!

One day I was reading my Bible and praying when I was impacted by a verse in Genesis.

> *'You intended to harm me, but God intended it for good to accomplish what is now being done, the saving of many lives.'*
>
> —Genesis 50:20

Joseph had managed to see God's plan in his life. Even though his brothers had meant to harm him, God had been powerful enough to orchestrate events so that many lives and, indeed, a whole nation would be saved through Joseph's experience. I thought of Pearl. The orphanage director had meant harm to her. But could God use her and us to save many lives through this experience?

I couldn't shake that vision and the thought that maybe the turnaround in her life could occur in others. As I once heard, "Only God can turn a mess into a message, a test into a testimony, a trial into a triumph, and a victim into a victory." I desperately wanted the lives of many HIV victims turned around to lives filled with victory.

One day I was speaking to our American friend, Justin, an HIV specialist who had worked in China for a number of years. He was the doctor who initially helped us get medication for Pearl. "I feel like I want to look after more orphans with HIV, but I don't know if that is what God wants." As usual I was waiting for a text message from God. "I don't even know how or where to start." As the words came out of my mouth, I realized that this was just another of my harebrained schemes.

"I tell you what," he said, "if you somehow get kids out of orphanages, then you will know that it is a miracle from God. The Chinese aren't proud of the children with HIV and certainly won't be looking for foreign help."

First, I was surprised that he didn't think it crazy at all. Second, I agreed with him. Staff, access to medicine, and money seemed nothing compared with the insurmountable task of actually finding these children. But God is bigger than any earthly struggle. "

> *'Commit your way to the Lord; trust in him and he will do this: He will make your righteousness shine like the dawn, the justice of your cause like the noonday sun.'*
>
> —Psalm 37:5–6

Six weeks later, at nine o'clock at night, we received an email that stopped us in our tracks and certainly changed the course of our time in China. Again!

"Dear all,

We are working here in Chongqing and have been asked to take two children aged between two and three years old who are HIV positive. They seem physically very well, but being only fairly recently abandoned they are withdrawn and depressed. They are isolated, and the orphanage staff has no wish to have any contact with them; the medical staff seems very ignorant of the facts regarding HIV/AIDS.

If we take them, it would not be an appropriate setting for them as we care for very sick/dying babies or children, though it would be better than where they are.

I'm wondering if you know of anyone working in China who would consider helping care for them."

We did not know the woman who sent the email, but friends in China, England, and America had forwarded it to us.

I read the email and then read it again. Was this the miracle we were talking about? I wanted to email the woman straightaway, but Sam, ever the sensible man, said to wait. We decided to pray about it and take things slowly. If it weren't for his wisdom, I would have gotten on the plane that night to pick up the children.

Over the next few days there was a flurry of emails between us and the English nurse who had first asked for help. She was running an inspiring home for orphans requiring palliative care- Butterfly Children's Hospice. Obviously the children she emailed about were not palliative-care material, so we hoped we would be able to find them a home and medication. The future certainly looked bleak for these little ones if they stayed where they were.

They had already spent six months in an isolation room, and the staff at the orphanage had no idea what to do with these children they considered highly infectious. Once again, the obstacles seemed insurmountable: orphans with HIV travelling across provinces, getting medication and medical appointments, finding them a home and a caregiver. My excitement deflated as I realized the enormity of the task ahead of us.

One rather large complicating factor was that the boys and I were returning to Australia in a few weeks to organize medical appointments, do some banking, and take a well-deserved break in the sun and surf, especially for the boys, who were once again missing Australia.

Sam and Pearl would stay in China, with extra help during the days so he could continue to work part-time. Even though we knew that being apart would be hard, we thought this was the best solution under the circumstances.

Over the next two weeks we made many phone calls and exchanged emails to sort out the future of these kids. Our children were very excited at the opportunity to welcome these children into our home. We had some fun conversations as to what we could call them. Kath and Kim was a popular choice when we thought they were both girls. R2 and D2 was another great suggestion from our boys who had just entered the Star Wars age. (Sam and I promised them we would consider all options!)

Two weeks after the first email and three days before leaving for Australia, I boarded a plane to bring these kids to our home. At the time the wait had felt like forever, but looking back, it was such a miracle that it all happened so quickly. Sam wrote about it in his supporters' letter:

"Things have happened so quickly here!!

At this moment, Julie is in another province, 800 km to the southeast of us, where two weeks ago an orphanage there discovered that two of their children have HIV, and via a British nurse working with them, a request for the care of these children went out across the country.

After some discussion, we gladly agreed to take these children into our home and spoke with the orphanage directors, who were just as keen for us to take care of these children.

So, probably later tonight, we will have five children under our roof!!! Thomas, James, Pearl and a two- and a three-year-old child, one boy and one girl. Julie and I are so excited to begin something that has been on our hearts for so long (almost eighteen months now!!).

We have already spoken with the HIV professor here who is very willing to sign the prescription that allows them to have life-long anti-HIV medications supplied free.

Now we plan to care for them in our family until we can rent another apartment and find a 'mama' to live with and care for them. From there, we will provide all medical care, social integration, and education—with the hope that they will be adopted in the future, with the best possible chance to live a long and disease-controlled life.

We would so love to set up a model and standard of care for these children, that the community and other care facilities can then see that this is not a disease to panic over but to love and nurture these children. In doing this, perhaps those yet-to-be-diagnosed children can receive proper medical care and remain with their biological families—ultimately a far better place than orphanages.

We are so grateful for the incredible response to our previous email for your assistance with this—not only was it rapid but extraordinarily generous.

What wonderful people we have to call friends from around the world."

So as Sam and the kids prepared our house in Xian, I packed my bags with spare clothing, nappies, much excitement, and a little trepidation to head off to Southern China and meet these two little ones.

R2 and D2, here we come!

Fourteen hours and many cups of Chinese tea later, I walked through our front door with two Chinese toddlers in tow. They were almost as exhausted as I was. The girl, whom we called Rose, woke briefly. She looked around her. Confusion clouded her face, then she screamed her lungs out—a scream we would soon grow used to as she threw her head back, closed her eyes, and let the whole neighborhood know of her distress.

The screaming woke Pearl, who blearily looked at the newcomer and asked the question on everyone's lips. "Where is her mama?" A question that all adoptive parents and children one day ask.

Where was her mama? Was she sick and maybe dying from untreated HIV? Was she lying in bed, wondering about the toddler she had left at a bus station six months earlier? Or had she given up hope that her little one would ever feel love and happiness again?

I wrote in my journal the next day.

"It has been a long day. Thankfully I can't imagine what it is like to deliver twins, but in a way I feel like I just have! I am exhausted.

I left with a bag full of baby clothes and nappies and arrived home eighteen hours later with two children. The first two of our HIV orphanage.

During those long eighteen hours, I took two plane flights, drank multiple cups of Chinese tea, shook numerous hands, filled out even more forms, and, of course, cuddled kids.

Luke, two and a half, met me with smiles and hugs, but his feelings changed rapidly when he realized that this crazy blue-eyed foreigner was taking him away from the room that had been his home for the past six months. He cried loudly and kicked and punched at me at the crowded boarding gate and then for the majority of the flight. People usually stared at me just because I was a foreigner, but the staring intensified at the sight of a stressed-looking foreigner trying to cope with a distraught two-year-old!

I disembarked feeling exhausted, embarrassed, and despondent. What on earth were we doing? Maybe all the people who thought we were crazy were right. Could we cope? Would I ever sleep again? Is this really God's will? Maybe we heard wrong.

As we sped through the empty city streets in our taxi, I wearily turned on my phone to check my messages. There was a text from my friend, Bev, in America: "I know God is smiling because of what you did today" and was followed by Isaiah 40:28–31.

> *'Do you not know? Have you not heard? The Lord is the everlasting God, the Creator of the ends of the earth. He will not grow tired or weary, and his understanding no one can fathom. He gives strength to the weary and increases the power of the weak. Even youths grow tired and weary, and young men stumble and fall; but those who hope in the Lord will renew their strength. They will soar on wings like eagles; they will run and not grow weary, they will walk and not be faint.'*

I sat back and leant against the window as Luke contentedly (finally) slept on my lap. I had somehow managed a huge day and had felt God's strength at every moment, every cup of tea, every minute of turbulence, and every tear from Luke. I thought of Luke, one of the weakest people in China. He was helpless and unwanted, yet God had promised to give him power. I thought of myself, probably one of the weariest Mums in China, and God had promised me strength. Together we were a living example of Isaiah 40:29 that night."

Chapter Sixteen

Gum Trees and Palm Trees

Over the next few days we struggled to manage five children, pack our bags for Australia, take the new children for medical appointments and blood tests, and say our good-byes to China. We were overwhelmed with support from the local expat community as people dropped by with toys, clothing, meals, and other delicious home-baked treats. We were also overwhelmed with attention from the locals as they saw us with not one but three Chinese children!

A 'quick' trip downstairs to the vegetable sellers became a mammoth effort with three sets of coats, scarves, and gloves to don, a double and single pram to tackle, and three pairs of reluctant feet to squeeze into shoes.

Despite the huge change in their lives, the newcomers settled in and their personalities quickly shone through. Rose was a happy little girl with a strong personality. She had no reservations about snatching away another child's toy and could cry loudly for what seemed like hours when she didn't get her own way. At less than three years of age, she was particular in what she would wear and was already refusing to wear clothes that were not pink. She loved to be cuddled and tickled and had the most gorgeous dimples when she smiled. She especially loved Sam and revelled in any attention from him.

Luke was a quiet little boy who coped admirably with being bossed around by the two girls. Both Pearl and Rose would often dominate him as they played together. When he was able to escape them, he was happy to sit in a corner and play with cars, look at books, or do a puzzle. His medical examination performed at the orphanage described him as having low IQ. I certainly felt that he was depressed and had been traumatized in his short life, but there was absolutely no indication that he was anything but very clever. He was quickly drawing, completing puzzles, and sorting shapes within a few days of arrival with us.

If we didn't change his environment he was happy, but he strongly resisted change as he had shown me on the first night on the plane. If we tried to take him outside or to another room, he would plant his feet on the floor and scream until we gave in.

After a few attempts at taking him on a walk, I was quickly tired of the curious onlookers staring at the foreigner trying to reason with a traumatized two-year-old. We all decided to stay indoors where it was warm, safe from the stares of strangers, and surrounded by an ever increasing supply of toys.

Both children, especially Luke, showed us the hoarding behaviour that is common in children recently removed from an orphanage. Often food is not given regularly, so when it is it is completely under control of orphanage staff rather than the child's hunger. It's not like the little ones can go to the pantry and say, "Mum, I'm hungry," raid the fridge like our children do, or throw a tantrum at the shops for a lollipop! These kids were fed on schedule and often went hungry in between. We learnt quickly not to have food on display, as it would suddenly disappear. I would change Luke's nappy and four mandarins would roll onto the floor! The decorative fruit bowl was quickly moved to a higher place, out of the reach of little hands.

Despite the odd fights, tantrums, and the never ending washing, cooking, and cleaning, the days were filled with happiness, cuddles, and laughs from all of the children.

The nights, however, were a different story.

As soon as bedtime approached, the kids would start screaming inconsolably. One of us would hold Luke, rocking him on the bed as he screamed and fought us. Finally, after forty-five minutes, his little body would go limp and he would drift to sleep, covered in sweat and tears.

Rose was not so 'easy.' For the first night she fought sleep with a level of tenacity I have never seen in a child. After an hour of crying, she fell asleep, only to waken with a start ten minutes later and commence the whole cycle again. That first night with us, she continued this until 5AM , when we finally got her to sleep by rocking her in the pram. Then Sam and I both fell into an exhausted sleep for the hour or so before the others awoke.

After a few of these long, exhausting nights, we began to wonder why these children feared sleep so much. Well, Sam did. I was too exhausted and frustrated and disheartened to even think. All I wanted is for the kids to sleep, not wonder why they would not. Sam kindly offered to watch football all night and hold Rose as she slept. As long as he held her, she remained relaxed and asleep.

"Why do you think she won't sleep?" he asked the next morning as the sun rose and all things seemed a little brighter. "She seems frightened."

As long as she was held, Rose would contentedly drift off to sleep, but at the smallest hint of being put to bed, she would instantly wake up and start the screaming. Even pulling all the mattresses into the lounge room and sleeping in bed with her would not settle her. We began to wonder about the circumstances of their abandonment.

We assumed that these children, close to three years old when relinquished, had recently been diagnosed as HIV positive—probably when they undertook the mandatory blood tests and medical examination required prior to entrance to preschool. Why else would parents raise a child for over two years and then abandon her?

These children, unlike Pearl, looked and acted completely healthy. They were both left in prominent places, likely in the hopes that they would be found, loved, and cared for—Luke beside a police station and Rose at a busy bus depot. How could parents leave a child, walk away, and the child not follow the parent?

A few months before I had met a child who was abandoned at three years of age at the orphanage gates. He had been bundled up in blankets with his legs tied together to ensure he did not follow his parents back home. But this was not the case with Luke and Rose.

Weeks later the truth dawned on me. The answer to Sam's questions hit me. Poor Rose was scared, terrified of being abandoned again!

I was sitting comfortably in my lounge room reading a book about orphans in India. It must have been the only book about orphans that I hadn't read. I read about how children in India were abandoned at markets, train stations, and even on trains as they slept. Parents would rock them to sleep and then disappear into the night. The poor child then would wake hours later . . . alone. Had Luke and Rose also been abandoned as they slept? Had they gone to sleep comfortably at a bus and police station in their parents' arms, only to waken hours later with no parents in sight?

We will never know what happened on those crisp autumn days when they were relinquished, but this scenario certainly would explain their fear of sleep.

I so wished I could have been there to hold and comfort Pearl, Luke, and Rose when they awoke, distraught to find themselves alone. I can only believe that God was there and heard their tears and brought them to us six months later. I can only believe that as they, like the psalmist, flooded the bed with weeping and grew weak with sorrow, God was there hearing and accepting their cries for mercy.

> *'I am worn out from groaning; all night long I flood my bed with weeping and drench my couch with tears. My eyes grow weak with sorrow; they fail because of all my foes. Away from me, all you who do evil, for the LORD has heard my weeping. The LORD has heard my cry for mercy; the LORD accepts my prayer.'*
>
> —Psalm 6:6–9

Homeward Bound

As the boys and I prepared to head back to Australia, the enormity of the task Sam had ahead of him as he single-handedly cared for three toddlers hit us. We organized some help for him so that he could still work part-time, shop, cook, and maybe even eat and sleep as he cared for three children under three. Two lovely Christian girls from a neighbouring village would work daily with Sam, cooking, cleaning, and entertaining the three youngsters. So the circumstances were not easy but were certainly manageable as the boys and I said a sad farewell to our growing family and headed for sunny Australia.

We had been in China for two years and leaving was more of a culture shock than we expected.

The boys were thrilled to experience a soft bed in Hong Kong and even more thrilled to board a Qantas plane filled with fellow foreigners. We rarely saw foreigners in our city of nine million, and the boys had become almost Chinese in the way they pointed and stared at white-skinned, yellow-haired people with blue eyes!

"Fish fingers!"

"Spaghetti bolognaise!"

They yelled in excitement as our in-flight meals were served. Were we the only people on the flight so excited to see the Western-style meal arrive? It was comparable to taking two starved children to a five-star banquet!

For the eight hour flight the boys revelled in the Western food and TV they could understand. As they sat back contentedly watching TV and playing video games, I looked out the window and wondered what it would be like being in Australia again, and, more important, I wondered how Sam and the kids were coping in China.

Just prior to arriving in Australia at 10PM, an announcement came over the loudspeaker that we would have to circle for ten minutes because of air traffic congestion. Apparently there had been a storm offshore, so there was now a queue of aircraft waiting to land. Ten minutes more seemed forever as we were all so excited to be on Aussie soil again.

Finally our plane landed then taxied to the gate. We gathered our belongings, eager to be back in Australia. After wearily navigating customs, passport control, and claiming our baggage, it hit us; we were in Australia.

There is nothing as comforting as hearing the customs official say, "G'day, mate," after a long flight and two years overseas. My excited parents met us at the airport, and we hurried to get into their car—our first with seat belts in two years—to drive the short distance to our accommodation in Sydney for the night.

As we stepped into the warm night air, Thomas (then nine) looked up at the night sky and said, his voice full of wonder, "Look, Nanny, at all the planes waiting to land." Thousands of lights lit up the Sydney night sky.

"They are stars, darling," my Mum replied with a smile.

Not long after, we arrived at our overnight accommodation, tired but excited. The boys started getting ready for bed. "Where do you get the water from?" they asked as they prepared to clean their teeth.

"The tap," my parents answered and looked at each other quizzically, probably wondering what on earth I had done to my children over the preceding years.

As I fell into an exhausted sleep, I considered how living in China had affected the boys. Two years is not a long time for adults, but for my young boys, they had forgotten what stars looked like and that it was safe to drink water from the tap in most countries.

There began five weeks of rediscovering the joys of living in Australia: sand, blue sky, sunsets, and grass you could walk on. But also freedom to say *church*, and *God* and even to pray in public. My boys and I learnt over those weeks, that Australia really is the lucky country!

> *'When I consider your heavens, the work of your fingers, the moon and the stars, which you have set in place, what is man that you are mindful of him, the son of man that you care for him'?*
>
> —Psalm 8:3–4

While the boys and I relaxed with family and became reacquainted with the 'good life', things weren't so easy or relaxing for poor Sam in China in the middle of winter with three young children. We spoke to them regularly on Skype and loved seeing the kids' smiles as they blossomed seemingly overnight from scared and lonely orphans to happy toddlers.

We enjoyed hearing the funny stories. Rose decorating all three of them with markers and Pearl teaching the others how to help themselves to the fridge!

The girls we had hired let them watch the same DVD ten times in a day after being told that the children could watch only one DVD a day. Apparently they took Sam's directions literally and thought that watching the same DVD over and over again was not a problem!

One day less than a week after I left China, Sam looked even more tired than usual. He told me sadly that the girls we had hired quit. He learnt that although they weren't fearful of HIV, their parents banned them from working with the children.

So Sam was home alone with three children.

He interviewed many people to help us care for these children. Again and again we heard the same stories as they said, "I want the job but my friends/husband/neighbours will disown me if I accept." All these Christians were apparently eager to serve God and their community but not risk the discrimination that would ensue.

Sam received wonderful help in the form of meals and child care from foreigners and some local friends; however, caring for three toddlers meant that he could no longer go to work, and in a country where we relied completely on the overcrowded public transport, shopping was almost impossible. But he continued to manage the kids patiently and calmly, in the way he approaches all things.

The photos of them at that time always show a smiling Sam and three happy, cuddly toddlers. Despite that the girls' clothing and hair weren't quite the way I would have liked, Sam did an amazing job. I could see that not only were the kids' physical scars from orphanage life healing but also their emotional ones. They giggled and laughed and loved to climb all over Sam as he tried to speak to us on Skype.

Although we loved being in Australia, we missed Pearl, Sam, and the two newcomers. James particularly missed China and felt very much an outsider in Australia. Even though he had just turned five when we'd left, to him China was home.

One day I left the boys, nine and seven, unattended in my parents' apartment while I hung the washing on the line downstairs. Ten minutes later I returned to a distraught James, who was on the phone with a police officer. Thomas had rung 000 to report me missing. After being chided by the officer for leaving the boys unattended, I hung up. I was confused and frustrated at Thomas's overreaction. "I leave you in our apartment in China all the time to get veggies and milk."

"But we have friends in China," James answered.

It was then that I realised that China was home to my boys ! Truth be told, we all were looking forward to seeing Sam and the kids again upon our return to China.

The week prior to our returning, Luke, Rose, Pearl, and Sam all became sick with high fevers, muscle aches and pains, and a cough. Sam managed to take the children to the hospital for X-rays, which were thankfully clear. They all survived what we later discovered was the swine flu. The boys and I returned home to a clean house, a tired, relieved, and slightly thinner husband, and three energetic and delightful toddlers. Sam had single-handedly cared for three children through Chinese New Year and the swine flu, and he'd come out almost unscathed. He certainly deserved a rest (and maybe sainthood)!

It was obvious to many that the strength Sam had over those five weeks as a single parent to three HIV-positive toddlers living in a foreign land was supernatural.

> *'It is God who arms me with strength and makes my way perfect. He makes my feet like the feet of a deer; he enables me to stand on the heights.'*
>
> —2 Samuel 22:33–34

The weeks and months flew by, and life in China seemed to get easier. As the ground gradually defrosted and we could shed a few layers of clothing, we all felt more positive about the future.

As the fruit trees blossomed outside our window so did Luke and Rose. They spoke more English and loved running outside to play hide-and-seek in the garden.

Every morning three toddlers woke us by running into our room with mischievous smiles on their faces. The morning ritual of breakfast, medicine, toileting, and dressing often took me until 10 AM!

Almost three months after we first brought Luke and Rose home, we finally found someone willing to care for them. Following a weekend of praying and fasting, a village girl accepted the job, and we moved them all into a nearby apartment. We are still humbled at how this girl had the strength and call to care for these children. She risked everything to do this, and it really was an act of faith on her part. If friends and family knew that she was living with children with HIV, she would be ostracized from the community. She would not be allowed to attend church, would never marry, and would even be disowned by her family.

It wasn't until later that we learnt how hard it was for her. Two years after moving in with the kids, she sent us an email telling how she felt during those first few weeks.

> "Before I look after them, I made up my mind that if God wants me to get HIV then I cannot escape no matter how hard I try. If *He* doesn't want me to, then I won't get that even if I live with them every day. I had much faith to HIM at that time.
>
> It was around 5 AM on May 5 when Luke woke me up. I was shocked and stunned by the scene in front of me: all his bed and pajamas were smeared with blood, and his nose was still bleeding. I couldn't wait to wear [put on] gloves and wiped blood with paper tissue. I've never seen a child's nose bleeding like this. Then I called Julie, and Julie said it was all right and then came over to help. She told me that Pearl was like that before. Luke's nose has bled for a dozen of times, among which there were five or six times very serious.
>
> But I had very bad dreams every night. I dreamt that I was infected with HIV, and all my friends, relatives, and everyone turned their backs to me, hit me, and threw things on me. I was really, really frightened by that and had less faith to Him not as before. Because I knew that the children need to have blood tests every couple of days, which I was afraid the most. Although I was a nurse and never would think twice before I give shots to other people."

Caring for orphans in Western society is a respected calling, and those who do this are looked up to. So many times people have told us that we are 'amazing', but we have been blessed with so much from equally amazing people in Australia, America, and Canada with gifts for the kids, prayers, and financial support. But to care for orphans in China is considered a sign of weakness. Even the Chinese church largely sees orphans as the rejected and unloved. Anyone willing to work with such children are automatically destroying any career and marriage prospects.

The heroes aren't the foreigners who live as expats and care for orphaned children. The real heroes are the millions of Chinese foster mamas who risk everything, including broken hearts, to care for these children as they wait for adoption. They live out what Mother Teresa advocated, "Let us touch the dying, the poor, the lonely and the unwanted according to the graces we have received and let us not be ashamed or slow to do the humble work."

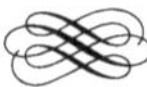

We thought long and hard about what possible names we could give our new venture to help children with HIV in China. I jokingly proposed Kangaroo Kids or even Vegemite Kids to reflect our Aussie background. Thomas and James continued to request a Star Wars theme, and Pearl and Rose wanted anything that involved flowers, butterflies, and the colours pink and purple. A Chinese friend suggested Elim Kids. Elim was where the Israelites rested whilst stumbling in the desert for forty years and just after the event at the bitter waters of Marah.

> *'Then they came to Elim, where there were twelve springs and seventy palm trees, and they camped there near the water.'*
>
> —Exodus 15:27

The name suited us perfectly because we would be providing these children with a resting place after the hard life in an institution and hopefully prior to the 'promised land' of adoption and family love.

The children moved into their new home on the first day of spring. Their building was surrounded by blossoms and spring blooms—almost as good as palm trees!

Chapter Seventeen

Too Much Turbulence

In May 2010 I received an email that chilled me to the bone.

It came from Pearl's orphanage director and said briefly, "Do you still want to adopt Pearl? We are preparing to send her file to Beijing."

I read the email a few times and tried to read between the lines. Why would the orphanage suddenly decide to send the file to Beijing? Once it arrived in Beijing, she could be adopted by anyone. The orphanage had always promised to keep her file until we were ready to proceed with our side of adoption. If her file went to Beijing, it would then probably be sent to America, where the majority of special needs children's files went.

We hadn't even started our adoption paperwork and assessments. We had a file already in Beijing, waiting for a healthy child. But as expats adopting a special needs child, we would have to start over, completing the entire process again.

We hadn't started the process for a number of reasons. First, we were waiting for her blood results to improve, and second, we had hoped to get a travel visa to take Pearl to Australia.

Deep down I had always been scared to start the process. I'd cheerfully say, "We plan to adopt Pearl" without any of the ensuing stress of actually having to fight for her. It would be a hard battle not only with the bureaucracy but also in dealing with discouragement and disheartenment throughout the arduous process.

Over the next few days I faced many personal moments of truth.

I had always maintained that although we desperately wanted Pearl in our family, I could cope with her going to another family as long as I knew she was loved and cared for. But when faced with the very real possibility of her being adopted by another family, I admitted, at least to myself, that I could not deal with saying good-bye to her, wondering every day if she was happy or felt rejected and abandoned by us. Every time I put her to bed, I imagined how hard it would be to put her to bed the last night before she went to another family. Every time I cleaned her room, I imagined how I would feel packing her dolls and clothes to go to another bedroom. Every time I made her favourite breakfast of a soft egg, tinned peaches, and 'freezing water', I would wonder if her new Mum would know what she needed and wanted.

And then on the other hand, I found it difficult to answer the many questions people posed: "Is she your child?" "She doesn't look like you." "Is she allowed to go back to your country?" Each time I was asked these questions I held her hand tightly and answered the best I could. But deep down I knew that she wasn't legally our child, so she couldn't return to our country with us.

I added a journal entry:

> "We just received an email asking if we still want to adopt Pearl.
>
> The orphanage is going to send her file to Beijing where she can be adopted by another family.
>
> I feel so sad at the thought of her leaving us. Sad for us but also sad for her.
>
> Who else will know that pink is her favourite colour? Who else will know that at bedtime you have to first sing 'Jesus Loves Me', followed by 'Baa Baa Black Sheep', and finish with 'The Rainbow Song'?"
>
> As I think about the long process ahead of us and the possibility of having to say good-bye to her, I turn to the Bible for what I hope is a quick answer.
>
> I read James 1:12, '*Blessed is the man who perseveres.*'
>
> And the next day I read Isaiah 1:17, '*Defend the cause of the fatherless.*'

> God has given me no quick answers or miracle cures for my despondency, but He has given me two words: *persevere* and *defend.*
>
> He has not guaranteed a yes to adoption, but I have hope that through social worker interviews, embassy phone calls, reams of paperwork, and more, He will be with me and give me the strength to indeed persevere and defend the cause of this special little girl.

As I pondered about Pearl's future with us, I remembered a Chinese proverb regarding the pearl: Pearls lie not on the seashore. If thou desirest one, thou must dive for it.

This proverb originated hundreds of years ago when all saltwater pearls were retrieved from the bottom of the ocean. To obtain a precious, valuable, and priceless pearl, the divers would have to rapidly descend to the bottom of the ocean, without the fancy diving apparatus that current day divers possess. Not only was great risk involved, but the diver had to persevere and persist, not knowing which shell would reveal the beautiful jewel. Not only would the diver be required to take risks and leave his comfort zone, but his patience and endurance would be tested too.

Risk taking, patience, and endurance were not at all my strong points. In fact, I often joked to friends that the biggest risk I would take was trying a new coffee shop! I knew, however, that like the diver, I would need to possess all three attitudes if I wanted to embark on the adoption journey to retrieve my precious pearl.

'Wait for the Lord; be strong and take heart and wait for the Lord.'

—Psalm 27:14

At this time Sam was in Australia for a few weeks, working and catching up with friends and family. Sam was usually the calm, practical one, while I was the one to panic and worry. If we were flying in a plane and began to experience turbulence, I would grip the armrests until my knuckles were white, whilst Sam, wearing headphones, sat obliviously watching a movie or sport. I would turn to him and mouth,

"Is everything okay?" No response, as he was captivated by the news or football scores. As the turbulence continued I would try again. "Are we going to be all right?" Still no response! With ongoing turbulence, I can cope no more. I take his headphones off and yell, for the whole plane to hear, "Are we going to crash?" at which point a surprised Sam would glance out the window, shake his head, and go back to TV watching.

This time my whole life felt buffeted by turbulence and Sam was not next to me. He wasn't there to glance out the window of my life and calmly reassure me that everything was okay. As I reflected on the situation and felt terribly alone, I saw that my whole life is like a flight. When there is no turbulence I sit back and relax, enjoy the on-board entertainment, sip the complimentary drinks, and snack on the food provided. "I deserve a break," I tell myself. "I deserve to enjoy myself a bit."

But the minute turbulence strikes, I dig desperately in the seat pocket, grab my Bible and prayer journal, and plead for safety and protection. That is so often how it is in my life. I am happy and comfortable to sit back and relax, calling out to God only during turbulence.

And now it felt like we were flying through a monsoon! I spent many hours in prayer, meditation, and Bible reading.

Not only was I trying to manage things alone in China and deal with the news about Pearl's file, but it seemed our whole family was plagued by illness, so I was up most nights with one child or another. Thomas had recently been diagnosed with Henoch-Schonlein purpura, an autoimmune disease causing a rash and joint pain. Although he had mostly recovered, he was still experiencing abdominal pain and kidney problems. All his symptoms seemed to flare the minute Sam boarded the plane for Australia.

At 2 AM on a cold snowy night, with Thomas sleeping fitfully beside me in between bouts of abdominal pain, I wrote these words:

> "My friends and I joke about TMC [too much China] days, but I am having a TMC week!

Sam is away and I am home alone with three kids. Home is not the word I would use to describe China at this moment because I feel very far from home.

So far I have had many sleepless nights with sick kids—croup, fevers, and severe abdominal pain.

It has rained constantly, and despite being a mid-spring it has even snowed. The government-supplied heat was turned off a month ago, so it is freezing cold, inside and out.

As the sleep deprivation accumulates, so do my fears and irrational thoughts. What if something serious happens? What do I do?

Where is God, and why isn't He listening to me? Am I being punished?

Why are my children suffering?

How on earth will I survive another three weeks like this?

I feel like every night I am up battling and pleading with God to help ease the suffering.

Help me have faith.

Help me praise You in the darkness.

How could You love Thomas so much, yet see him in this pain?

Help me use this experience to depend on You more and also encourage the children to depend on You.

What are You trying to teach me? Faith? Perseverance? Trust?"

Thomas's pain finally eased and he fell into an exhausted sleep. I sat up, wide awake and running on the adrenaline of fear and worry. After writing, I read my latest Max Lucado study and one sentence comforted and challenged me. "Faith is knowing that God is real and God is good."

I hardly ever doubted the reality of God. Just looking at creation and the intricate workings of the human body daily reminded me that there was a higher being. But how often did I doubt that God was good? When I saw homeless people freezing on the streets, when I heard news of war, car crashes, and earthquakes, and when my children suffered!

As C. S. Lewis said, "God whispers to us in our pleasures, speaks to us in our conscience, but shouts in our pains: It is his megaphone to rouse a deaf world."

I sometimes wish He would turn the 'megaphone' down a bit. I have listened to as many sermons and read as many books on suffering as the next person, yet I am still no closer to an answer. All I could do on those long nights was to trust what God tells me in Psalm 62:11–12: '*One thing God has spoken, two things have I heard: that you, O God, are strong, and that you, O Lord, are loving.*'

While in Australia, Sam supported me via multiple phone calls and emails, and he even managed to contact the adoption social worker. We had arranged to get our home study completed as expats, so Sam returned to China armed with our wedding certificate, police clearance, and other vital documents. Not to mention chocolate, vegemite, coffee, and toys!

The kids and I had survived a multitude of illnesses, and with the return to normalcy, I was reassured that God does answer our prayers. I had asked that God could help me use the hard times to bring the kids to a closer relationship and dependence on Him. Sometimes they remind me to depend on Him:

> "Last week Pearl complained of a sore tummy. Immediately she was barraged with questions from Dr. Mum. Where is it sore? How long? Do you have diarrhoea? What did you eat for lunch?
>
> Of course, I examined her, getting her to hop on each foot, and checked her urine and temperature.
>
> After patiently answering these and more questions, she said, "Mum, can you just say a prayer?"
>
> So I humbly tried to put away my anxious mother/doctor role and said a prayer for the sore tummy. She awoke the next morning pain-free and full of energy. To her my power is not in being a doctor but a Mum who can pray.
>
> And that is how we are with all we do in China. Our power is not in our medical training, ability to raise funds, or navigate the Chinese

medical system. Our power is in prayer. James 5:16 says, '*The prayer of a righteous man is powerful and effective.*'

Again and again it has been the kids who have reminded me of the power of prayer. Instead of running around with jelly, thermometers, and wet washers for James, he says to me, "Can you say a prayer?" When Thomas is bullied at school and I am tempted to ring every teacher and parent involved, he says, "Should we say a prayer?" When Pearl is awake all night with a croupy cough and I am attacking her with nose drops, antibiotics, ventolin, and vaporizers, she says between bouts, "Should we ask God to take the cough away?"

'Only be careful, and watch yourselves closely so that you do not forget the things your eyes have seen or let them slip from your heart as long as you live. Teach them to your children and to their children after them.'

—Deuteronomy 4:9

Chapter Eighteen

Lucy

After Luke and Rose left us, it was strangely peaceful to go back to having only three kids in our home.

We missed Luke and Rose but were fortunate to see them every day because their caregivers looked after Pearl while I homeschooled the boys. Sometimes I would look out the kitchen window and see a loving ' 'mama' pushing two toddlers on the swings as they all laughed and squealed in delight. When the children would turn their chubby faces toward me, and I would see that they were Luke and Rose, such joy arose within me that I had mistaken them for just two other Chinese children. Despite their disease and abandonment, they were beginning to fit into a culture that never wanted or accepted them.

We looked after Luke and Rose on weekends so their caretaker could have some time off. When they came over, we loved watching them run into the house with squeals of delight as they helped themselves to every toy and book.

Nearing the two-year anniversary of our arrival in China, we were happy that we had been able to help at least three children go from an orphanage to a loving family situation.

But the future didn't look great for Luke and Rose. Their caregiver was often in tears as she told us that because of their disease, they would never be able to attend school, get a job, or get married. What hope did they have?

We tried to reassure her that God did have a plan for them, but deep down we also worried. How would they be educated? How would they survive? Had we been impulsive, impatient foreigners taking on these kids when we didn't fully understand the reality of the future they faced? To our knowledge, no HIV-positive children had ever been adopted out of China, so the prospects seemed poor for them.

We committed to just take one day at a time, and their caregiver faithfully prayed every day and night that one day they would have parents.

We tried to teach people regarding the facts about HIV. Both foreigners and Chinese had little knowledge about the virus, and most of what they believed was untrue, so we ran education sessions to dispel some of the common myths. I was shocked to discover that many people still thought that HIV was God's judgment and that the children deserved the disease because they were being punished for the sins of the parents.

We will never know why our kids' parents had HIV. Where they prostitutes? IV drug users? Or where they poor peasants and farmers who sold blood and tragically contracted HIV through their simple effort to earn 55 yuan (less than AU$10) and a bag of eggs?

During the early 1990s, businessmen and government workers began buying blood from poor villagers, especially those living in Henan province. Not only were they using inadequate screening techniques, but the blood was being pooled and then re-transfused into the villagers so they could donate again soon. Subsequently, HIV rapidly spread throughout whole villages. The Chinese government later admitted that between 30,000 and 50,000 people were infected this way, although some sources believe that the true number is probably more.

Regardless of how they contracted the disease, Luke, Rose, and Pearl were innocent children. They loved to play hide and seek, have bubble baths, and play with playdoh and bubbles, like every other three-year–old anywhere in the world. They certainly didn't deserve the prejudice and discrimination they received.

One day Luke and Rose's caregiver told me how God had spoken to her the previous night. She admitted that she often still feared contracting HIV and was especially scared when the children had bleeding noses or cuts.

As she was putting Luke to bed, singing a song and saying a prayer, she suddenly recalled the verse in the book of John about the children suffering, not because of sin, but so that God's glory might be shown.

> *'As he went along, he saw a man blind from birth. His disciples asked him, 'Rabbi, who sinned, this man or his parents, that he was born blind?' 'Neither this man nor his parents sinned,' said Jesus, 'but this happened so that the work of God might be displayed in his life.'*
>
> —John 9:1–3

Tears ran down her face as she told me that she wanted these children and their lives to glorify God, and that she would devote herself to them to making that a reality. She was certainly true to her promise. By the age of three, Luke, Rose, and Pearl could quote Psalm 1 and 23 in Chinese. They would remind us whenever we forgot to say grace before a meal, and they loved entertaining visitors by singing 'Jesus Loves Me' and Psalm 42 in Chinese.

They were also well loved at the Chinese and foreign churches they attended and at their foreign preschool. They prayed honestly every night for others in distress, their own adoptions, and their friends. Their caregiver even had them giving out Bible verses to the doctors and nurses in the hospital where they received medical care! This was something that I would never be brave enough to do!

There was no doubt that they were giving glory to God.

> *'From the lips of children and infants you have ordained praise because of your enemies, to silence the foe and the avenger.'*
>
> —Psalm 8:2

Meeting Lucy

Over the next few months we gradually became acquainted with the Chinese doctors who dispensed the HIV medicine. It was clear that they thought we were crazy and had no idea what we were dealing with. They were not at all impressed when we altered the children's medication dosages according to each child's weight.

One day the doctor, feeling very kind, warned me (via a translator) of the dangers of working with HIV. "The foreigners do know they shouldn't prepare meals together in the same dish as the children? They realize that if they share chopsticks they may also get HIV?"

I felt like exploding but patiently explained to this doctor that we were not in any way worried about catching the disease from chopsticks or cooking utensils. I felt like we were banging our heads against the wall. Would we ever change people's wrong thinking about this disease? If the doctors working in the infectious disease hospital thought that HIV was transmitted by sharing food, how on earth could we convince the general population otherwise?

We were surprised then, when these people contacted us and asked us to help an HIV-positive eight-year-old girl. She and her very frail mother lived an isolated life not far from us.

I was slowly learning to be patient with all things Chinese, so after a month and many e-mails, phone calls, and meetings, we were allowed to meet this little girl and her mother. We were in the middle of another very busy 'Bring Me Hope' camp, so we decided that she and her Mum could come and visit camp for a day or two. They would have plenty to do and it would be good for her to meet us in such a fun environment.

I will never forget the first time I saw this frail, thin, dirty girl pushing her Mum's wheelchair. Both of them were so thin, had multiple sores covering their skin, and had months of caked-on dirt over their bodies.

When Pearl first saw them, she froze, staring at them in shock. It was obvious to even the non-medically trained among us that the mother was extremely unwell and didn't have much time left on earth. I gently held Pearl's hand and encouraged her not to stare. I glanced down at her. To imagine this plump little toddler with glossy hair and rosy cheeks ending up as a wasted woman in a wheelchair was too hard to bear. Even though they shared the same disease and attached stigma, their lives were worlds apart.

The little girl, whom we named Lucy, hung back, reluctant to play with the other children. We later learnt that she had been locked inside for nearly two years. If she did manage to go outside, the local children called her names and threw rocks at her because of her disease.

Gradually, and with much coaxing, she joined a game played with balloons. Within a few minutes she was smiling and jumping with the other kids. I glanced down at her mother and noticed tears running down her face, leaving dirty streaks trailing down her cheeks. I then looked at my other friends and fellow volunteers, and they, too, had tears running down their faces. We all stood together and watched in amazement as this eight-year-old social outcast became just another kid waiting for a turn.

Lucy and her Mum stayed at camp for two days. We gradually grew to know and love them.

Lucy loved craft and swimming, hugs and dancing. Her whole face lit up when anyone came to her and touched her or danced with her. Within twenty-four hours of arrival, she changed from a scared little girl who hid behind her Mum's wheelchair to an outgoing little princess with a giggle and hug for everyone. Staff and volunteers alike fell in love with her and were amazed at her transformation. That she had no positive human contact in the past two years was nothing less than tragic. She reminded me of the leper in the Bible who was healed by Jesus's touch and compassion.

The more we worked with HIV-infected people in China, the more we noticed the similarities between modern day HIV in China and leprosy worldwide. The words of Mother Teresa rang true with the people we were encountering. "The biggest disease today is not leprosy or tuberculosis, but rather the feeling of being unwanted."

Sadly, she was so right. The main disease wasn't the overwhelming viral loads or lack of healthy immune cells, but the devastating loneliness and lack of fulfilling and loving relationships.

We knew we couldn't heal Lucy or her Mum's HIV, but all of us who had fallen in love with them vowed we would try to cure their loneliness.

Toward the end of their stay at camp, we were all saddened to send them away from our hotel and back to their small apartment. Someone suggested that we bless them by going to their house and clean it, paint their nails, and maybe help prepare a meal. Initially the mama was reluctant to accept our offers of help, but with many reassurances that this was often done in our home countries and that we actually wanted to help her, she agreed to let us visit.

So the next day we packed our bleach, garbage bags, and nail polish for a girls' day out. All the volunteers planned to spend the morning pampering Lucy and her Mum and then relax together with KFC for lunch and a cheap manicure.

We climbed the dirty cement stairs in their apartment block. When Lucy answered the door, both she and her Mum greeted us with big smiles and hugs. We gave Lucy's Mum the English name Christina.

It was hard to hide our shock when we saw the state of the apartment. Dirt coated the rough cement floors. A rotten cabbage covered with flies was the only food visible, and it was obvious by the state of the toilet that they had no running water. The bedroom was filthy, and human waste stood on the floor beside the bed, obviously there from the times that Christina didn't get up to go to the bathroom. We expected a rat to run out of the bedroom at any moment as we gingerly walked around trying to conceal our horror.

Despite that it was midsummer it was cold in the apartment. I perused the main room, looking for evidence of a heating system. I found none because they had no heat of any kind. I wondered how these two survived the bitter winters where it is below freezing for at least two months.

None of us had ever experienced such poverty and filth.

We were beginning to realize that Lucy's Mum was suffering from AIDS-related dementia and the effects of an old stroke. At thirty-two years old, she was unable to care for herself, let alone her daughter. Lucy, at age eight, was completely responsible for food preparation, helping her mother into the wheelchair and to the toilet, cleaning and organizing the apartment. I am sure my house would look similar if I left my eight-year-old in charge for two years.

We resolutely put down our buckets and mops and got to work. We knew that hours of work wouldn't begin to scratch the surface but resolved to try our hardest to show we cared. One of the volunteers played with Lucy, drawing and making necklaces. Another opened the nail polish and started to clean, cut, and paint Christina's nails. My friend Natalie and I donned gloves, got out the bleach, and started scrubbing years of filth from the kitchen. She and I chatted and commiserated on how hard their lives were and how little we could do to help. Occasionally I would glance over at Cathy, who sat calmly painting nails and listening to worship music. I didn't envy her. There was no way I could clean such filthy nails without showing my disgust. I was so thankful for gloves and bleach! Cathy told me later how lucky she felt and how glad she was that she didn't have to clean the kitchen. We all laughed at how God has made us all so different, yet we can all serve in such varying ways.

After a few hours of work we were all exhausted, but we had made only a small difference. Once again there were tears of gratitude as we said our good-byes. Christina and Lucy waved to us from the window as we walked down the hill to the bus stop.

I wondered when they would next have a visitor. If ever!

We were all quiet on the bus trip back to our hotel. Everyone was thinking of what they had just seen and experienced, and feeling helpless. How could innocent people suffer so much? How could we help? Occasionally, I caught the eye of another volunteer and noticed tears forming in their eyes, as they were in mine.

We were subdued as we ate lunch, and then we went to have our manicures, which are cheap in China—about AU$7 for a great manicure, complete with flowers and glitter; however, the excitement of such a bargain was dulled by the knowledge that we were probably spending more on our nails than Lucy and Christina had for food for a week.

Over the next few months we learnt more and more about the lives of these two precious people. It was like peeling back the layers of an onion—a very bad onion. Their horrific experiences could fill a book. Unfortunately, I am sure that this story is repeated throughout China and the world countless times.

Christina contracted HIV from her husband. When Lucy was born, he was so angry that she was not a boy that he broke Christina's arm and left them. She was left alone to care for and raise her baby, who also was HIV infected. Lucy never went to school. We are still unsure why but suspect that she was not allowed to attend because of her disease.

Christina's condition continued to deteriorate as she lost weight and succumbed to repeated opportunistic infections. When Lucy was only six years old, Christina suffered a massive stroke, for which she was hospitalized for many months. Miraculously, she regained the ability to eat, drink, and sit up, but remained unable to walk or coordinate her right arm. She had also been diagnosed with AIDS-related dementia.

Devastatingly, she and her daughter's 'new' diagnosis of HIV led to them being more socially isolated. Christina's brother was ashamed and scared for his safety and that of his young family. He bought a cheap apartment in the outer suburbs and moved them into it. He employed a man to care for them. He paid this complete stranger 1000 yuan (about AU$180) a month. This evil man then promptly pocketed the majority of the money he received. He physically and verbally abused both Christina and Lucy. It is likely that their being HIV positive is all that protected them from being sexually abused as well.

In order to manipulate and control them, this wicked man would let them go for days without water and electricity. He would withhold their medication from them as a punishment for perceived bad behaviour and would give them one cabbage, a small amount of rice, and a few pieces of old bread per week.

He also regularly employed prostitutes behind his wife's back by using Lucy's bedroom to entertain them. We shuddered to think about what this eight-year-old girl had been exposed to and experienced.

Because of their disease, Lucy and her Mum were despised by the local community. Their neighbours locked them in the apartment for two years and plugged the keyhole so they couldn't escape. They also taped their apartment door shut and regularly doused it with insecticide in a bid to prevent the virus from 'escaping' into the apartment block.

Subsequently, prior to meeting us, their only human contact was the three monthly visits by the representatives from CDC (Centre for Disease Control and Prevention) to dispense medication and perform blood tests. The locals would even try to stop them from visiting, barricading their cars and banging on the doors and windows repeatedly, begging them to remove Lucy and Christina from their community.

Sam and I were shocked every time we heard a new revelation about how much this mother and daughter had suffered. In our sheltered lives we had only read in books and viewed in movies about people being treated so badly. To actually hear it and witness it with our own eyes was sometimes too much to bear. Many times I would return home from visiting them dejected and disheartened by the treatment they were receiving. I would tell our Chinese staff all the horrible things the neighbors were up to.

One day Luke and Rose's caregiver surprised me by defending Lucy's neighbours. "They are not bad people," she assured me. "Most Chinese people are the same. Our neighbours would do the same if they knew that Pearl, Luke, and Rose had HIV."

I shuddered to think that we were so close to being treated as outcasts. In our relatively wealthy neighbourhood, we were treated like royalty. The children were usually dressed beautifully in foreign clothes, and people would stare in wonder as they heard Pearl speaking fluent English. I was often asked which English language school I was sending her to!

We resolved to do all we could to help Christina and Lucy. It was an overwhelming and daunting task, but we were comforted that God had heard their cries and was lifting them from the dirt and dust they were living in.

Over the next few months, with the help of our foreign friends and amazing Chinese volunteers, we cleaned a room that could be used for Lucy's schoolroom and employed a tutor for her. We organized a roster so that people would regularly visit and help with cooking, cleaning, and overseeing medication use.

Lucy was also welcomed and loved by the local Chinese church, whose members didn't know the disease she was harbouring but saw her simply as a child who needed love.

Lucy and her Mum's lives were still far below what even the poorest people in the West cope with, but gradually we were making changes.

> *'Because of the oppression of the weak and the groaning of the needy, I will now arise,' says the* LORD. *'I will protect them from those who malign them.'*
>
> —Psalm 12:5

Chapter Nineteen

Waiting . . . Worrying

In May 2010 we nervously embarked on the adoption journey. Four years after we submitted our file for a 'healthy child', we started preparing our paperwork to request a specific child with HIV. It seemed like an impossible task ahead of us.

We emailed all our family, friends, and supporters about our decision and asked for prayer. We knew we needed it! One response hit home. "Nothing will test your faith and reliance on God more than the adoption journey." I already knew that to be true.

As we had our home study, submitted bank statements, and did criminal records checks, Pearl's orphanage was preparing her medical notes, abandonment certificate, and photos. Our social worker assessment went smoothly and we managed to gather all our paperwork together. Miraculously we lodged our application just three months after starting the process.

We were delighted to receive a supporting letter from the Australian government stating that they would allow Pearl to become Australian regardless of her medical condition. We were shocked, however, to receive another letter from Australia stating that the health waiver for her visa to enter Australia would be over half a million dollars.

Sam and I assumed that this would be the price we personally had to pay for her to enter Australia. Neither of us panicked because at this stage we believed that money would never be an obstacle between us and Pearl. She would indeed be our 'pearl of great price', for we would choose her over all the riches in the world. Sam and I recalled his dream of a few years ago. We would sell the house, work locum shifts, and ask for donations.

I must admit, however, that we were greatly relieved to discover weeks later that we both had misread the email and wouldn't need to sell all we owned after all. We realized after speaking to officials at the Australian Embassy, that once adopted her disease would be 'costed' to ascertain how much her medical care would cost the Australian Government. If the cost was over a certain limit we would then have to apply for medical waiver in order to be granted citizenship.

Erroneously interpreting that first e mail however had made us both realize that money would never be an object to us adopting her. A price cannot be placed on a cherished family member!

All we needed now was Pearl's file to be submitted, with a letter from the local Civil Affairs office stating that it recommended us as her family. And, voila, the adoption would be complete!

Easier said than done!

We comforted ourselves knowing that our file was safely locked in the central adoption offices in Beijing while the orphanage was still preparing her file.

One day we were asked to submit passport-size photos for her file. I joked to Sam that we didn't want her to look too cute lest someone else would want her, but she needed to look well cared for and loved by her foster family. I quickly did her hair and we went downstairs to the local photo/photocopy/printer shop.

I knew the owners well from all the previous paperwork they had copied for us. I suspect they had read enough of her file to know that she had HIV, but they mentioned it to no one. They would always put down their cigarettes and give her a big hug and tell her how beautiful she was.

This was our Chinese community. The man who swept the courtyard, the lady who sold me milk, and the few veggie sellers who dotted the streets were always happy to see me and patiently listened to my horrid Chinese, nodding and smiling all the time.

Strange as it may sound, it was these people I missed when I returned to Australia. It is hard to fathom that as we travel around the world, see new and different people, and go through a multitude of experiences, these people unobtrusively became a part of our lives, faithfully printing photos, sweeping floors, and selling veggies—contributing in myriad ways to making our lives better.

Once again the winter drew near, and temperatures and moods plummeted.

I began to daily hope that the mail run would produce Pearl's file and an invitation to adopt her. It had been a long four months since our paperwork had been lodged in Beijing. Even though we were told twelve months was the approximate waiting time, I was really hoping and praying that it would be sooner.

Every time I walked the fifteen-minute hike to collect our mail, my heart would be in my mouth. Would today be the day? How would we celebrate? Would it be with noodles, rice, or dumplings? Or would we spend up big and take the kids to McDonald's to celebrate? Who would we ring first?

I was always disappointed to receive more school work (as were the boys), and even packages bearing chocolate and vegemite seemed a disappointment compared to adopting Pearl.

Just prior to Christmas we decided to have a family holiday on the idyllic Hainan Island. Not only did it offer sun, surf, and blue skies, but we figured that it was the closest we could get to Australia without leaving China.

We had enough frequent flyer points, so after numerous phone calls we booked our flights and accommodation. We were off to our seaside holiday!

We could hardly wait to get on with our holiday. Each day our eager anticipation of soaking in some sunshine and just resting from the daily routine grew. I visualized lying on a lounge reading my book whilst sipping coffee, the boys visualized playing on the beach and swimming in the pool, and Sam looked forward to a break from work. Pearl had no idea what to imagine but she was excited anyway!

The day before leaving, the orphanage contacted us. "Could you please arrange for Pearl to have a test for syphilis so that we have it for her file?"

Aaaagh! They had no idea what their request did to us. This meant that Pearl's file hadn't even left the orphanage! All those anxious trips to collect the mail had been in vain. There was no way we could be matched with her when her file wasn't even in Beijing.

We rushed to get her tests completed and sent to the orphanage. I tried to look at the bright side that at least I could have a complete break from every day wondering if today would be the day.

We boarded the flight with our bags packed with swimmers, towels, and expectations of a great, if short, family holiday.

We arrived at Sanya airport at 3 AM. The kids managed to sleep through the transfer to the courtesy car, which took us to our hotel, and getting to our room. Even then they didn't awaken, so we were able to get them into their beds before Sam and I fell into bed ourselves.

The next morning we awoke to screams of delight.

"We have a TV in our bedroom!" Thomas said.

"We have Foxtel!" James added.

"We are in Australia!" Pearl said as she danced around the room.

We opened the heavy plush curtains to a spectacular view of green grass, blue sky, and the glistening ocean. To one little three-year-old girl we were indeed in Australia.

We had a wonderful few days of sun, surf, and fine food. The children loved being free to swim, run on the grass, and eat Western-style food. Pearl made her first sand castle, and Thomas and James quickly regained their love of swimming. Sam and I relaxed away from the stresses of work, adoption drama, and constant emails. We almost felt like we were back in Australian as we sat on the hotel balcony overlooking clear water and feasting on *real* pizza!

Though not totally cut from our lives in China, we did check our emails once. After opening one, Sam yelled at me in excitement. Good friends of ours had been successfully matched with their special needs foster son.

Our file had been lodged at the Centre for Adoption Affairs on the same day as theirs had. I would love to say how I celebrated with them and jumped for joy at their wonderful news. I would love to say that I acted in the biblical way of rejoicing when a brother rejoices. But the truth is that I burst into tears! A look of astonishment chased away

Sam's excitement. After fifteen years of marriage he still couldn't figure me out.

"What about us?" I lamented. "It's not fair. What have we done wrong?"

All I could think of was how this family was rejoicing whilst Pearl's file was still sitting on someone's desk in the orphanage.

After I calmed down with the help of an 'all you can eat' breakfast and cup of coffee, I sat on our balcony overlooking the ocean and read my Bible. Its words could have been right out of my mouth.

> *'How long, O LORD must I call out for help but you do not listen? . . . Why do you make me look at injustice? Why do you tolerate wrong?'*
>
> —Habakkuk 1:2–3

As I sat and pondered those words, I had to admit that I wasn't the first in the world to see injustice. The injustice I felt was nothing compared to the 147 million orphans worldwide who went to bed every night without the love of a family.

I was encouraged by part of God's answer in chapter 2: '*Though it linger, wait for it. It will certainly come and not delay*' (v. 3). I really hoped and prayed that the answer to our adopting her would be as soon as possible. I didn't think I could cope with another delay.

The next day I was walking along the beach with Pearl when one of the waitresses from our hotel stopped us. Once again the same line of questioning ensued. "Where is your mama?" she asked. Pearl gave her the "you really have no idea how stupid you are" look that only a three-year-old can give and get away with. She pointed to me and said loudly in Chinese, "This is my mama."

I smiled and kept walking to avoid any further questions.

I reflected on what life was to Pearl. She didn't need paperwork, passports, or files to be matched. To her young mind, we were in Australia and I was her mama.

As we packed our bags to return home, I reflected on how through the hard times God had been with me. A friend of mine on the fostering/adoption journey described it perfectly: "It's this never ending cycle for me these days. I struggle, I doubt, I cry. Then *He* shows up. I remember,

I see, I believe. It's not an accident. I am where I am supposed to be . . . He isn't finished with me yet." We returned home refreshed, warmed, and ready for another Christmas in China.

Christmas in China was a great way in teaching us to improvise. We put up a second-hand (or was it third-hand?) Christmas tree. Unfortunately, the top had fallen off, so we rigged an ingenious concoction of chopsticks and Blue-Tack to keep it upright. We dusted off the few Christmas ornaments we had been given. The kids decorated the house with pieces of tinsel and snowflakes they cut from white paper.

We had no decorations related to Jesus and the real meaning of Christmas, so we made salt-dough Christmas decorations and painted them with nail polish. For us that year, the smell of Christmas wasn't cinnamon and peppermint, but pungent nail polish! We certainly wouldn't have won any home beautiful awards. I even enjoyed baking three cookies at a time in my small toaster oven!

Though we were excited about Christmas, our hearts went out to those who had no heat or Christmas joy. Lucy, and her foster Mum came to mind. Our Chinese friend who was tutoring Lucy told us how unbearably cold it was in her house. They had no heat, and the concrete floors seemed to radiate the cold. They had little food and certainly no Christmas decorations to cheer them up.

The boys and I went to visit them one day. A fifteen-minute taxi ride took us to another world, it seemed. Their house was so cold inside that the toilet water had frozen! The food that we could see was covered in flies and maggots. It was obvious that they hadn't eaten for a few days.

Despite their hardship they greeted us with big smiles and hugs. The boys and Lucy went outside to make snowballs whilst I chatted to her Mum and foraged for a way we could give them food. The boys were horrified at their situation and tried to think of solutions. Lucy's Mum was reluctant to move, which left them both hungry dirty, and cold. We decided that Lucy would come to our house three days a week for tutoring. Our Chinese friend could tutor her in the warmth of Pearl's pink room filled with toys, photos, and clothing.

The first time Lucy came to our house she was amazed at the extravagance of our small three-bedroom apartment. She walked around in awe as she looked at the toys, curtains, and Christmas decorations.

She hungrily ate a huge bowl of noodles, after which I gave her a bath. Because their house was so cold and had no hot water, Lucy hadn't had a bath for over three months. So I encouraged her to take off her many layers of filthy clothes as I ran the 'bath.'

We didn't have a bath in China. They were actually very rare so we had bought a big washing basin and would fill that with warm water for the kids. I filled it with warm soapy water and showed Lucy the bath toys.

Who would ever have thought that a bath would be such a joyous occasion? She stayed in the water for half an hour, giggling and squealing as she played with the bubbles and poured water from one toy to another. I suspect this was her first bubble bath with toys.

I dressed her in some clean clothes that had been donated for her, including a purple sparkly top, which she loved. The transformation was amazing. She and I had enjoyed her makeover so much.

That Christmas was so different from our Australian Christmases. It snowed heavily on Christmas Eve and the kids delighted in playing outside, making snowballs and snowmen. We invited good friends to share a large bucket of KFC for lunch.

The contrasts of these Australian and Chinese countries were amazing: snow instead of sand, KFC instead of turkey and ham, and homemade decorations instead of the beautiful glass ones that were packed away back in Australia. But our Christmas in China was made special as we remembered the joy of Lucy's first bath and seeing Luke and Rose experience their first Christmas. Only one thing dampened the otherwise festive mood: that Pearl, who was spending her third Christmas morning with us, was still not officially our daughter.

The ultimate rich man, Jesus Christ, became poor for you.
That means that we ought to be deeply involved in the lives of
broken people in this city. And it means not just giving your charity,
giving your money, though that's very important.
But it means giving your time, giving your relationship.
—Tim Keller

A Trip to Henan.

In the heart of winter I received an email regarding a foster home in the neighbouring province. On a whim I replied and congratulated the woman who ran it on her amazing work. I also mentioned the HIV work we were doing and suggested she contact me if she knew of any HIV-positive orphans who needed care.

Within minutes she replied that she was being visited by an American Adoption Agency particularly interested in helping children with HIV. After a flurry of excited emails between her, me, and the agency itself, we decided that I would travel *the next day* to meet them and share about the work we were doing. The first email had arrived at 8 AM and by 1 PM I had tickets booked to travel via high speed train to the neighbouring province.

In retrospect it was probably one of the bravest and craziest things I ever did. I didn't even have time to think of all that could go wrong as I travelled across China the week before Chinese New Year.

The next afternoon I arrived at the high speed train station two hours early. It had been in operation for a only week and the heating had yet to be installed. No amount of chocolate eating and foot stamping could warm me up as I paced the deserted railway station.

Just before the train arrived, Sam rang me with good news and bad news. The good news was that Pearl's file had finally arrived in Beijing. The bad news was that it had arrived without the crucial letter stating that she should be matched with us.

As I sped along the frozen Chinese countryside at 240 km per hour, I was once again plagued by 'what if'?

What if her file was already in America?

What if the head of Civil Affairs didn't write the letter in time?

What if she gets matched with another family and the whole matter is out of our control?

I couldn't help but worry. In *Fresh Wind, Fresh Fire*, Jim Cymbala wrote, 'Prayer cannot truly be taught . . . It has to be born out of a whole environment of felt need. If I say 'I ought to pray' I will soon run out of motivation and quit . . . I have to be driven to pray.' So I pulled out my notebook and prayed. I wrote furiously for two hours as I prayed protection over her file. I prayed that God's angels would surround her file and that He would keep her a part of our family.

Throughout the weekend unbidden mental pictures flashed through my mind. I would see Pearl's file being whisked off to another family. Then I would pray and plead with God like I never had before. Once, I prayed that God would speak to me audibly and comfort me that things would be okay. I received no reply, leaving me disheartened and exhausted.

Little did I know that He was speaking to someone on the other side of the world on my behalf.

Despite the fear and worry hanging over my head, I managed to enjoy the weekend as I visited children in a few small foster homes and then toured Maria's Big House of Hope in Luoyang. I was encouraged to see that whether it was in the sparkling new rooms in Maria's house, or in a cold cramped apartment, these children were being loved and cared for. I was comforted watching these children smile and laugh as they played with their caregivers and waited for their forever families to collect them.

Sometimes the statistics were discouraging. How could there be 147 million orphans worldwide going to bed every night without a family? That number, four times Australia's total population, was impossible for me to grasp.

I would so often think of Pearl, Luke, and Rose. Though they were only three lives out of 147 million, I could not imagine a day passing without seeing their smiles and cheeky personalities.

Two days after arriving in Zheng Zhou I battled the crowds, purchased a ticket home, and whizzed once again across the snow-covered landscape toward home.

I walked in the door at home and found Sam busy on the phone. Over the weekend he had sprung into action and rung everyone possible to discuss Pearl's file and lack of accompanying letter. Unfortunately it was a week before Chinese New Year, when the whole country stops for three weeks to eat dumplings and set off fireworks. Though everything came to a screeching standstill in China for the festivities, America did not. If her file did indeed go to America, Pearl could at any moment easily be matched with a family.

The orphanage directors whom Sam spoke with promised that they would do all they could. I didn't get my hopes up, despite repeated assurances not to worry. I felt so frustrated and angry that someone not completing his or her paperwork could change our lives. And Pearl's!

Once again I reached for my journal to help me sort through my thoughts.

January 2011

Every day feels like a thousand as we wait for news on adopting Pearl. My brain is filled with questions. Where is her file? Where is ours? What is taking so long? Has something gone wrong?

When the mail arrives, I walk the icy streets to the office with a heart filled with a mixture of hope, dread, fear, and anticipation.

I walk home with a heavy heart, as yet another day goes by without the arrival of the document.

Another foster Mum and I were recently talking about the foster-adoption waiting process. She said that she felt consumed by the wait. This is exactly how I feel. I am consumed daily by the wait and not knowing what the future holds for Pearl and me.

This week I was reminded of two verses I learnt in my early days in China when I was feeling overwhelmed by killer viruses, poisoned milk, and earthquakes.

'Because of the Lord's great love we are not consumed, for his compassions never fail. I say to myself, 'The Lord is my portion; therefore I will wait for him."

—Lamentations 3:22, 24

It dawned upon me that I need to be consumed, not by Pearl and the waiting process, but by God and His love for me and her.

I have now changed my prayers and asked my friends to change theirs. I am praying that I am no longer consumed by the process but consumed by God.

Two days later I added:

"I still think, worry, and wonder about her adoption, but God has released me from being consumed by it. I am able to go for days at a time without focusing on the wait. I am able to trust in the Lord's timing and that He is in control and that His love for me never ends."

'Now may the Lord of peace himself give you peace at all times and in every way. The Lord be with all of you.'

—2 Thessalonians 3:16

I resigned myself to another long wait as China closed down for the festivities. Lack of this one vital letter stopped the entire process, meaning that we would not hear anything about Pearl's adoption for at least a few weeks. Once again the 'princes' of China had let us down.

'It is better to take refuge in the LORD than to trust in man. It is better to take refuge in the LORD than to trust in princes.'

—Psalm 118:8–9

Chapter Twenty

Happy Chinese New Year

February 1, the day before Chinese New Year, Sam became unwell with the flu. He languished in bed, sipping lemon tea and warmed with a hot pack as I home schooled the boys. We were frantically trying to get ahead with school work because experience had taught us that the coming sleep deprivation caused by the constant overnight fireworks would make concentrating on school work difficult.

I was on my way to drop off a friend's birthday present when our company office called to tell us we had a letter. So once again I traipsed over the icy roads up to the office. This would be my last chance to collect mail for a few weeks, as the whole of China closed down to celebrate New Year.

Although the air was cold, it was one of those rare days when the sun shone through the pollution. Looking up to see the sun, I felt its warmth on my face. It was so rare for the sunlight to pierce the pollution that while we were back in Australia for a visit, James was surprised to see shadows. "Look, Mum! When I wave, so does the shadow!"

As I trudged to the office, I watched with interest as people were readying themselves for Chinese New Year. The parks were clean, owners had swept and polished their shop fronts, and children ran around proudly holding boxes of fireworks. Old and young men, children and women were balancing precariously on ladders, stools, and scaffolding as they hung their red lanterns over homes and shop fronts.

I reached our office building and impatiently waited for the elevator. I boarded it and rode the twenty-six floors to our company office. *How many times will I ride this elevator with fear and anticipation in my heart?* I wondered. *Will it one day just be a normal activity rather than one that sends my heart racing and makes my mouth go dry?*

Sam had already warned me not to get my hopes up. "I am waiting for an important document from Australia. And there is no way the piece of mail there will be Pearl's file. The Chinese government official hasn't even written the letter yet."

So it was with thoughts of dumplings to prepare and fireworks to avoid that I entered the office.

Sitting on the office desk was a priority mail envelope addressed to us. I still knew not to get my hopes up, as I had recently experienced disappointment at the hands of a priority mail letter. It could be as uninspiring as someone's blood test results or more paperwork for us to complete. Maybe an application to join our company, or a completed medical examination for us to file! Yet how could I truly not hope?

I exchanged pleasantries with the office staff, all the while my heart raced and my hands itched to open the envelope.

I left the office and headed for the elevator. Whilst waiting for the lumbering elevator, with shaking hands I tore into the envelope. A photo of Pearl in a fairy dress we had taken a year ago fell out.

This was it! A letter to offer us the option of adopting a little girl from Hanzhong, whom we had loved as a daughter and sister for the past two and a half years!

My legs wouldn't hold me. I plopped down at the top of the stairs, amidst cigarette butts and trash, and cried with relief and joy and unbridled thankfulness. When I could compose myself enough to talk, I rang Sam. "We have a daughter!"

I resolved there and then to turn this blessing back to praise, for:

> *'Every good and perfect gift is from above, coming down from the Father of the heavenly lights, who does not change like shifting shadows.'*
>
> —James 1:17

The rest of the day was a happy blur of text messages, emails, and phone calls as we shared the exciting news with friends and family throughout the world. So many people shared our joy and relief and gave thanks for the many hours of answered prayer. Again and again we praised God for the miracle of this child becoming our daughter.

It was not until later that evening, when the three kids were fast asleep, that Sam and I were able to really talk. It was then that I learnt of the magnitude of the miracle.

"I have a story to tell you," Sam said. Though he looked solemn, nothing could dampen my excitement as I waited for him to explain.

"Our worst nightmare did come true." He held my hand. "Pearl's file did make it to America, and it was given to another family."

I stared at her photo and the adoption papers in disbelief. How could her file be in my hands then? What had happened? I sat down to steady myself as Sam told me the story.

A week prior, Sam had woken in the middle of the night and felt the need to check the emails. He found one from a woman in America who had Pearl's file sitting on her kitchen table.

We cannot thank this amazing woman and God enough for how she listened to His prompting:

> "You can't know how I have begged Father for the email to go through. I am praying that Father will make a way as He is the way maker. I will get right to the point.
>
> I have Pearl's file.
>
> It was totally a God thing. Wednesday evening of last week just before I went to bed, I checked my email and had two messages from two friends who do not know each other, but they both know me and my passion for orphans who are HIV positive. They both gave me the same information, that a U.S. agency has the files of three positive children waiting in China. I had to knock on the door.
>
> I asked my hubby who sighed HEAVILY before saying okay.
>
> Anyway, they have two children in a different part of the country than you are in—one boy and one girl, both currently three years old, and a girl, well, exactly where you are and, in fact, living with you!
>
> I asked only for the boy's file, as people tend to be drawn more to girls, and the boys so often get left behind.

Anyway, after I asked the agency for the boy's file I had a strong prompting to call back and ask for the girl's files as well. When I did, I was told that the other girl (not Pearl) was being considered by another family, so I said, fine, just send me the files that are NOT being considered yet by other families. And I found Pearl.

When I read the info about how she was living with a foster family from Australia who are doctors, well something inside of me spurred me on . . . a sense of urgency and I didn't even know why. Initially I thought maybe Father was about to do a miracle and we were going to be going back there to adopt another daughter.

I contacted an Australian friend of mine who is living in Hong Kong. I asked her if she knew anything about two doctors living in China. She said she did know of you two, but her memory was rusty and she had to go digging for info. She got back to me within an hour with links to news articles about you, the email address, and blog of Elim Kids.

The more I prayed and the more I read, I found a blog entry that mentioned a home study and you wanting to adopt Pearl.

My heart broke.

Here I was holding all of her information and photos and then finding your photo album. It was obvious that she is already part of your family and a treasured part at that . . . and to know that if we let her file go, then another family could easily commit to her and in a handful of months show up with all proper papers and take her away from home.

I could weep. thinking about this almost four-year-old girl having to leave.

Sam, is there ANY way you and Julie can legally add her to your family? I am certain there is a desire, but is there a legal reason why you cannot?

Is there ANYTHING, anything, ANYTHING I can do to help you guys before another family says yes and it is too late?"

Sam had replied immediately, stating that yes we certainly did want to adopt her and we would do anything to be able to get her file back from America and into our hands.

Her reply came almost immediately.

> "I am praying that Father would open doors that no man can close on behalf of your family and sweet Pearl. I cannot believe that of all the people in the States, I got her file first and the Holy Spirit has done all the rest . . . it really was an act of God finding you! So keep remembering that He is sovereign and His plans are good.

Two days later, this wonderful woman had been thrilled to receive this email from her American agency.

> "I do not have a copy of your number on hand but wanted to tell you that Mr. L informed me that the foster family has applied to adopt this girl, so the CCAA is allowing that family to proceed. I'm sorry your family will be unable to apply for her; however, it is great she will be able to remain in the family she has been living with. If you have any questions please let me know. Again, I'm sorry this child is not available now."

Both Sam and this American woman had rejoiced that Pearl would be soon ours. It was only another five days later that I received the file containing the fairy photo.

In his final email to her, Sam had explained perfectly how much we loved Pearl:

> "I just don't know what to write. I have been sitting here at the computer just reading your email over and over again and trying to take it in. Long pause . . . Still thinking . . . praising . . . His mighty right hand . . . His Father's heart . . . His provision for us all, for Pearl. This story will be always to the praise of His name. I am so incredibly grateful to you. You will never believe how much.

> There is always the title 'foster parents', that some people tend to put the emphasis on the 'foster' part . . . but these children are in our hearts and minds, our children. It cannot be otherwise when you have cared for a child for two years."

After Sam told me the story, I felt a range of emotions: relief, thanks, fear, and overwhelming gratitude. It took me a few days to fully grasp the reality of this miracle. Our princess's file had been sitting on someone's kitchen table on the other side of the world. This person *happened* to be a Christian and *happened* to know someone in Hong Kong who *happened* to have heard of us. That this woman felt a sense of urgency to contact us amazed me. The days when she felt the strong desire to look for Pearl's file and start searching for us were the days when I was visiting Zheng Zhou praying that angels would protect her file and crying out to hear God's voice. I am glad that she was listening and He spoke to her.

As William Temple said four hundred years ago, "When I pray, coincidences happen, and when I don't, they don't."

That was the first night in many months that I couldn't sleep, not because of fear and worry, but because of joy and thanksgiving.

> *'You have filled my heart with greater joy than when their grain and new wine abound.*
>
> *I will lie down and sleep in peace, for you alone, O Lord, make me dwell in safety.'*
>
> —Psalm 4:7–8

We continued to go through the motions of daily life in China and braced ourselves for yet another Chinese New Year. I busied myself stocking up with food and daily necessities for the break. Much to my dismay, Sam busied himself with stocking up with fireworks!

We enjoyed all the excitement. People set off fireworks from their apartment windows and in any spare piece of land available. With so many fireworks going off in a constant stream, the reverberations from the loud booms shook our building. Every family in China saved all year to buy fireworks for this special display that turned midnight as bright as broad daylight.

Day one of the ten-day celebration was fun, but by the last night we were pretty happy that the festivities were over and we could go back to normal life—fireworks only two or three times a day.

Chapter Twenty-One

Adoption

We eagerly contacted the local authorities and the orphanage and 'booked in' for the official adoption in three weeks, which is when we would sign all the legal paperwork and get Pearl's passport. Then she would legally by ours.

Then our next step would be to apply for her Australian residency. After the adoption she would indeed officially be our child, but she wouldn't be an Australian resident or citizen; however, the Chinese government would immediately cancel her Chinese citizenship, leaving her in a kind of limbo, a child with no country to call her own.

Despite that she spoke Chinese fluently and loved rice and dumplings, she would no longer be Chinese. Despite that she had an Aussie accent, could sing 'Kookaburra sits in an old gum tree', and loved vegemite, she would not be an Aussie. It was ironic, but after all we had experienced this was the least of our problems. So Sam busied himself again filling in documents and writing emails so we could begin the Australian application.

As the adoption day loomed and Sam continued to bury himself in paperwork, Pearl and I focused on more important things . . . what would we wear? She wanted to wear her pink Barbie dress with ruffled sleeves and endless butterflies and frills, but it was still very cold in China. That outfit was more suitable for a birthday party in Hawaii than adoption in Xian in the dead of winter.

Finally we settled on a navy blue dress.

I convinced her that she could still wear pink jewelry and a pink shirt, so she was reasonably happy. (I am sure wardrobe negotiations won't be so easy when she is a teenager.)

Two days before the adoption, I sat at the dining room table eating lunch with a friend when Sam unexpectedly early came home from work. His looked announced his anger, a look we hardly ever see. In fact, the last time I saw that face was the day in 2008 when the orphanage told us they would not accept Pearl back.

His voice quivered when he told me that Civil Affairs had decided to cancel the adoption. Apparently, before they would allow us to adopt Pearl, they wanted a guarantee by the Australian government that it would accept her—a guarantee that Australia wasn't willing to give until Pearl was legally the 'child of Australian citizens.' Then and only then would the Department of Immigration assess her application.

We were shattered. Once again the finish line had been snatched from us and we were so close.

I cried as Pearl and the boys looked on in horror.

"Mums don't cry," she said. "Only kids cry." She rushed into her bedroom to get me her pink blanket and teddy bear to comfort me. How could I explain to her that once again we needed to pray for favour so that we could adopt her? How could I tell her that once again she wasn't ours?

Over the weekend Sam frantically phoned everyone we knew in Australia who could support our case: our local member, lawyers, doctors, the Department of Immigration, and the Department of Community services.

They were all amazingly supportive and wrote letters to substantiate our case. All we had to do was try to convince the Chinese authorities. Sadly, we knew from experience, that arguments that make sense to us don't always win approval in a Communist country.

Whilst Sam was busy 'doing something' as his male brain dictated, I retreated to bed for the weekend with my Bible, books, and a large quantity of chocolate. I needed supernatural (and sugar-coated) strength to survive that weekend.

Sam continued to reassure me. "Do you really think that God would retrieve her file way from America only to let us down at the last minute?" Sometimes I had his faith, but other times I was filled with doubt. If God really was so powerful and loving, why didn't He prevent this from happening at all? I am sure that I am not the first, or the last, person to ask that question!

I was currently reading the book of Esther, although I never expected too much in the way of support and guidance. But as I read the story, it became clear that in many ways Esther's story mirrored Pearl's: an insignificant orphan who changed the hearts and minds of kings. Could the king in China in 2011 be the head of Civil Affairs? Could a little girl really make a difference?

I particularly liked 4:14. '*And who knows but that you have come to royal position for such a time as this'?* I clung to the thought that the little girl we often called 'princess' may indeed be able to change the heart of the 'king.'

Two days later as I was in the middle of spelling words and long division, I received a call from Sam. His excitement electrified me. "Get yourself and Pearl dressed and ready. We have a meeting with the head of Civil Affairs in one hour."

One hour? It would take at least half an hour to get to the Civil Affairs office, so that meant we had less than half an hour to get ready! I assumed that it would be best not to go in my home schooling 'uniform' - a tracksuit and old jumper. Quickly I made myself presentable and grabbed Pearl's blue dress that we had originally prepared for the adoption.

We hurtled through the streets of Xian in a taxi, my whole body shaking and my palms slick with sweat. Yet Pearl calmly chatted beside me.

My fear dissipated slightly when we walked into the shabby Civil Affairs office and I noticed that the man who would determine our future was sitting on a chair with a Mickey Mouse pillow!

Sam was already there, armed with a folder full of letters about our case. He was prepared to present them one by one.

The official, however, beckoned us to sit down. He spoke to Pearl in Chinese. "How old are you?"; "What is your name?"; "Do you like your Mum and Dad and brothers?"

Pearl politely answered. She stood and walked to him, offering to share her food with him. Not only did he take the food, but he actually touched her.

You could have pushed Sam and me over with a feather. Deep down we suspected that much of the reluctance regarding the adoption was that she was HIV positive. I am sure he imagined a frail dying child rather than a chatty four-year-old sporting a pink and purple necklace and a packet of chips.

After a lot of chatting on his part and smiling and nodding on ours (fortunately for all of us, we had a translator with us), he said that indeed we could adopt her . . . "and, by the way, would you mind in the future training orphanage staff to care for special needs children?"

We couldn't agree more quickly or excitedly. We set the adoption date and then left the office. Out on the street, amidst the incessant honking horns and street sellers shouting their goods, we remembered Sam's folder full of 'evidence' that we deserved to adopt Pearl. The man who decided our fate didn't need to be convinced by any paperwork; rather, chatting with Pearl and seeing her in person was enough. It was as Proverbs 21:1 says, '*The king's heart is in the hand of the* Lord*; he directs it like a watercourse wherever he pleases.*'

Once again our friends and family rejoiced with us and praised God for hearing our prayers. One friend's email particularly encouraged us. It expresses our feelings and emotions so precisely:

"Your three days of not knowing how this story would turn out makes me think of the disciples after Jesus's death and before His resurrection, and then His resurrection— to go from the absolute depths of despair and wondering what Father was doing to be transported to overwhelming joy and jubilation."

Two weeks later the little girl we had taken in to help her die became our daughter.

Not long after we adopted her, Pearl asked, "Should we adopt James too?"

We all laughed, realizing that she has felt part of our family ever since that first night on our bedroom floor.

The last two years of paperwork, waiting, praying and hoping had not affected her at all. In her mind, once she entered the door of our home that first day, she had entered our lives, becoming our daughter as much as James and Thomas are our sons. And together we are family.

Good-bye R2 and D2

Ten days after we received the documents that we were matched with Pearl, we were excited to receive the following e mail.

"Dear Julie and Sam:

You don't know me, but my husband and I have been following your blog for the last few weeks.

We have been looking into adoption and trying to discern God's call for us as to what country, what age, etc. We started out with one specific idea in mind, and then, as time went on, with faith and prayer, our parameters opened up and we waited.

Then we were shown Rose's file, and immediately my husband and I both felt that exact same strong, deep, heartfelt yearning to adopt her.

This feels so funny/strange to be writing in an e-mail and without ever having met. I just couldn't wait any longer to reach out to you in case we could start communicating. I also have been told that discretion is of the utmost importance when it comes to adoption in China, so I hope I am not overstepping or asking too much. Please forgive me if I have.

I know from what we've read, Rose is a part of your family, and since receiving her file, we've just been wondering every day how she is doing and what she is doing, and also thinking of you all and praying for the work you do, your family, the kids' caregiver/foster mom, and for Rose, Pearl, and Luke. It means so much to us to have the possibility to connect with you now. We hope, God willing, that the adoption will move forward and that we can stay in close contact throughout the years."

This amazing family, upon learning about Luke, proceeded to adopt him as well. I realized that the other two children the American woman who had received Pearl's file spoke of in her email were actually Luke and Rose! Miraculously, against all odds, they were adopted together as siblings. Luke and Rose were no longer feared children, stashed in an isolation room, who had no hope, but were now treasured children, siblings, grandchildren, cousins, and classmates.

We loved being the bridge between them and their forever family. What a privilege it was for me to race to their apartment and announce, "Luke, Rose, you have a Mum and Dad and big sister!" How lucky I was to be the first one to see big smiles spread across their little faces and Rose's dimples grow even larger. I had such joy in showing them photos of their new house and parents. Their Chinese caregiver was absolutely amazing once again. Even though she was sad at having to say good-bye to the children she had lived with and taken care of for two years, she was happy and relieved for the children and embraced their future with them. She delighted as much as they did when opening parcels from their new family. And she helped the children speak to their parents on Skype.

She wrote to their American Mum:

"We went to visit a friend of Luke and Rose's after lunch. When we came back at about 7 PM, we saw a parcel in our living room. I thought that might be from you. Luke and Rose can't wait to open it. Luke said, "My Mum is so great! I'm so happy with the gift!" Rose loves that dress the best. When I read your letter to them, we all cried and laughed. I told them that your baba and mama love both of you deeply. Since our first Skype, Rose knows that her older sister is at school and prays for her every night. Your letter was long and I read it three times for them. It seemed that Luke understood a lot after that. We sat on the floor and read for the first time; then we sat in the dining room for the second and third times. Luke sat on the table and Rose was in my lap. We cried and cried until someone outside hit the ground and we were all startled. Luke said, "What's wrong with us?"

Thanks a lot for the gift you gave me. It's true that God looks after every nest!"

On the first of February, Pearl, Luke, and Rose faced unknown futures in China, a country that passionately feared them and their disease. Less than three weeks later, all three of them had been matched with forever families, whom they will bless more than they can imagine.

However, as it is written:

> *'No eye has seen, no ear has heard, no mind has conceived what God has prepared for those who love him.'*
>
> —1 Corinthians 2:9

Chapter Twenty-Two

Homeward Bound

Six months after her adoption, we took Pearl and the boys home to Australia.

I am still not a lover of flying and intensely dislike turbulence but can in all honesty say that over the past four years of my life in China, I have again and again seen evidence of God's power and love—enough to help me cope with any turbulence, either on land or at 5000 feet above sea level!

> *'The* Lord *your God is with you, he is mighty to save. He will take great delight in you, he will quiet you with his love, he will rejoice over you with singing."*
>
> —Zephaniah 3:17

We were all so excited and thankful to be able to return home and show Pearl the country she had heard so much about.

Prior to leaving for Australia we asked what she wanted to do upon arrival. She had three requests:

To meet her cousins
To build a sand castle
To see God

Like many three-year-olds, she had her own theology. I have friends who have children who were convinced that the Easter bunny died on the cross or that it was the tooth fairy who told Mary she was with child. Pearl firmly believes that Jesus died, went to heaven, and then went to Australia. She was pretty excited to meet Him after all this time. I joked with one of my friends about how Pearl wanted to 'see God' in Australia, and she replied, "I think you have over the last three years."

She is right. Through the Tupperware family and the Chinese foster families, through the miracles in Pearl's life, and the smiles on the kids' faces at camp, we have seen God again and again. We have seen His love for the fatherless, His ability to do the impossible for them, and His love for the alien who can't even order a birthday cake!

I prayed that when we returned to our too comfortable lives in Australia that we wouldn't stop seeing God and His love for the orphan. I prayed that we never take our children, our safety, our food and clothing, and our country for granted.

And I prayed that we don't forget the orphans who are still there and their parents who have had to relinquish them.

America

Prior to returning to Australia, we spent a few weeks in America. It had always been Sam's dream to rent a RV and travel through America, visiting Washington DC, Niagara Falls, and more. It would be our first stress-free family holiday with Pearl. Travelling in China had never been relaxing because of the language and cultural barriers.

We also had many new friends in America whom we wanted to meet. We looked forward to finally meeting our amazing friends from Project Hopeful, an organization advocating for HIV-positive orphans. We wanted to visit friends who had adopted many of the children we had met at orphanages and camp and even the woman who had worked so hard to give Pearl's file back to us. We especially anticipated meeting and spending a few days with the waiting parents of Luke and Rose.

As the plane departed Beijing and flew thousands of meters over China, we unsuccessfully tried to crush Pearl's medication into her food. The air hostess rudely snapped at us when we asked for yoghurt. With great dismay (more for some than others) we learnt that we would have no audio-visual entertainment on the fifteen-hour flight. Nothing, however, could dampen our excitement as we realized that we were taking our daughter out of her country for the first time.

We had a wonderful family holiday, complete with s'mores around the campfire, visiting the famous Alamo, and touring Washington DC. We also loved meeting the many people whom we knew only through emails and the occasional Skype call. Even though we hadn't previously met any of these people, we shared a common passion for orphans, and they felt like family to us.

It was so encouraging to see the other side of adoption. For three years we had seen kids in orphanages awaiting their forever families. Now we were seeing them as precious and valued family members.

One such family had adopted a little girl from the orphanage we had first visited. After speaking to her Mum, I discovered that this little girl was one of the twenty crying babies in the very first room we walked into. Now she was a bright and bubbly four-year-old who entertained Pearl with her toys, dress-up clothes, and doll collection. She was very much loved by her parents and sisters.

Just prior to our leaving them, she and Pearl dressed up in pink dresses and gave us a 'concert' that only four-year-old girls can give. One girl singing with an Australian accent and the other with an American one, these little Chinese girls delighted us with a selection of nursery rhymes and praise songs. It was hard to believe that these two happy and well-adjusted girls had been lying forlornly and hopeless in orphanages just four years prior.

During our time in America we met so many adoptive families that Pearl must have thought that every family had an adopted Chinese child. One of the last families we met was the woman who had helped us retrieve Pearl's file. She had an adopted boy about the same age as Pearl, and she had two older children. Their recently adopted little girl was on the other side of the country with her Dad having surgery.

It was exciting and surreal to meet the family that could have been Pearl's. We saw the kitchen table where Pearl's file sat for those days whilst the family fasted and prayed over whether she would be their next daughter. We saw the bedroom that would have been hers.

After a quick chat we decided to go to an indoor kids play area. That way the kids could play and the parents could actually have a conversation! So off we set them in their car and us in our trusty RV. On the way through the busy streets, Thomas piped up from the backseat. "Pearl would really have liked it in this family."

I shuddered at the thought but had to agree. Pearl would have indeed thrived in this loving Christian family.

We arrived ten minutes later to the fun park. Thomas's words still echoed in my heart as I bought a cappuccino and settled in for a chat. Pearl, confident as ever ran off, hand in hand, with her new friend.

Half an hour later, my attention was drawn to Pearl, who had bravely climbed to the top of the slide but was not brave enough to come down. No amount of coaxing from the woman I was visiting with, her son, or Thomas would convince her that it was safe. I stood at the bottom of the slide, and with her eyes locked on me she gingerly edged her way to safety at the bottom of the slide.

Yes, she could have been part of another family, but in her mind, she was and always will be part of ours. It was my face that she needed to see at the end of the slide, at the school concert, and when she was unwell. It was our family that she needed to be with forever.

Three weeks after arriving in America, it was time to leave, time to say sad good-byes to all our newfound American friends and finally board the flight for the destination we had been waiting on for years: Sydney, Australia.

Pearl would soon meet her cousins, build sand castles, and be part of our lives in Australia.

What was meant to be a fourteen-hour flight morphed into more than twenty-four hours, as our plane stood grounded nearly fourteen hours in Fiji to refuel and await a new crew. We sat for many hours in the hot and steamy airport, wearing our winter clothing. Despite the obvious disappointment and inconveniences, we were still excited to be so close to Aussie soil.

Thomas and James were delighted to hungrily munch on twisties and lamingtons again, whilst Sam and I took turns sleeping on the waiting rooms chairs. Pearl spotted some noodles and, in true Chinese style, squatted on the food hall chair and devoured a huge plate.

Finally, twenty-seven hours after boarding our flight in America, we landed on our beloved Australian soil, with three unconscious children and five suitcases.

We took great joy in the spring weather in Australia, meeting cousins, and reuniting with friends. Pearl delighted in making her first Aussie sand castle three days after arriving in Australia and was enthralled by the kookaburras, magpies, and lorikeets that surrounded us wherever we went. She was relieved not to see a crocodile or shark. The boys amazed me with how quickly and easily they settled into Australian life. Some days it seemed as if we had never left. They happily played with their old friends, and for the first few weeks rarely mentioned China. They learnt to play backyard cricket and enjoyed many Aussie barbecues. Often they seemed like just regular Aussie boys, but sometimes they didn't.

Thomas, learning to backstroke during one of his first swimming lessons, stopped mid-stroke. "Mum, look at the sky!"

I looked up to a beautiful sunset of pinks and purples. I think the instructor was a bit amazed that she had to admonish an eleven-year-old for admiring the sunset rather than concentrating on the lesson.

We hadn't seen sunsets, rainbows, or even the moon for four years. Singing 'Twinkle Twinkle Little Star' in China had seemed a bit nonsensical.

One day we went to a friend's house for dinner. The boys loved the backyard and balcony but were particularly impressed with the kids' room set up with TV, DVD player, and toys.

"How many kids do they have?" James asked on the way home.

When I told him two, he was surprised. "That is a way too fancy and big house for just two kids."

It took both boys a few weeks to realize that it was okay to run on the grass but not okay to slurp noodles or leave your chicken bones on the tablecloth, not to mention going to the toilet on the side of the road.

Reentry for me was surprisingly difficult. I hadn't read any of the many books about 'reverse culture shock', naively believing it wouldn't—couldn't!—happen to me, for I had been wanting to leave

China for the last few years! I would just be happy and relieved to be home.

Although I was happy to go shopping, to the hairdresser, and to the post office without the fear of a language barrier, I struggled with people's comments about our time in China. Some friends were amazingly supportive and seemed to understand what we had been through and appreciated how we had changed. People who had visited us especially understood; however, many others didn't know what to say. I cringed as I remembered all the inappropriate comments I had made in the past to returning missionaries. Now after being on the receiving end, I know never to say:

"I bet you just loved every minute of it."

"Wow. That must make you feel really good about yourself."

"You've done your stint. Now you can settle back into life."

"You can't save the world, you know."

"Why China? Children suffer here too."

"I would never go to China. Have you heard what the government is like?"

"How was your holiday?"

When any of these things were said to me, I would force a smile. Then with as much restraint as I could muster, I'd answer them that during my China 'holiday I had seen malnourished orphans die, who in no way chose the government they lived under.

I did not feel good about myself as I settled back into a home that was at least ten times as big as many of my Chinese friends' apartments. I did not feel that my 'stint' was over and hoped that as long as there were orphans and poverty in the world, it never would be. I was painfully aware that I couldn't save the world, but then I would look at Pearl and imagine what our lives would have been without her and wonder how many more Pearls were out there waiting to bless a family.

I began to spend time with a friend who had just recently returned from ten years living in Papua, New Guinea. Even though our experiences were worlds apart, we both felt the same as we tried to fit into a country that no longer felt like home. Despite years of being the odd one out on the other side of the world, we suddenly felt like the odd ones out back home. We laughed together as we filled in the forms for the school swimming and carnival. Could our children swim fifty meters?

"I doubt it," I commented. "They haven't swum for nearly four years."

"How far is fifty meters?" she asked. "Mine can swim across the river in our village."

Even filling in a form was a challenge, not to mention working out school uniforms, library days, and school excursions, all those events that didn't occur in the home schooling calendar.

The foreigner who couldn't manage to order a birthday cake in China was now unable to go grocery shopping in Australia. I had to restrain myself from pushing past people like I did in China to get into the shops. I had to remind myself that in this country, we wait for the trolley rather than pushing and grabbing, which was the only way to survive in China.

On entry to the shops I was overwhelmed by the choices: twenty different yogurts rather than only three; vegetables and fruit neatly stacked in rows and costing at least five times that of the veggie carts on my street in China; the deli supplied chicken, cold meats, and salads but no live eels, bullfrogs, and turtles like the delis in China. After navigating my way through the centre of the store, I had to check out, and that's where the challenges really started. What was my pin number? I hadn't used it in four years. Do I swipe or insert my card? Which way does it go? Not only that, but they had these new self-service checkouts, where people priced and packed their own groceries. I avoided them for the first few months.

One day my friend and I sat sipping our cafe lattes, discussing all the challenges we were facing. Once again we wondered what we were here for. I reminded myself that there were good works just around the corner that he had planned for us. We also talked about how hard it was not to be the people constantly talking about what we had seen and experienced. "I don't want to be the annoying person who talks about PNG [Papua, New Guinea] all the time," she lamented.

I knew exactly what she meant. I felt like I was driving my friends crazy with my constant talk about China and orphans. I remembered back to an entry in my prayer journal of over a year ago. It convinced me, once again, that I was not to worry about what people thought of me but only of what God had planned for me. Maybe the good works He had planned was to spread the word amongst Australians regarding what was happening in the rest of the world.

December 2010

Luke 8:39: '*Return home and tell how much God has done for you.' So the man went away and told all over town how much Jesus had done for him.'*

Lord, I pray that when we return home we can give all glory to You. I pray that the words that come from my mouth can be glorifying to You and from your Holy Spirit. I pray that people's hearts can be softened and we can share with them all we have seen and all You have done.

> *'He is your praise; he is your God, who performed for you those great and awesome wonders you saw with your own eyes.'*
>
> —Deuteronomy 10:21

Pearl in Australia

On our Western-style automatic defrosting fridge in our home in Australia is a picture of the boys, Sam, and me on our way to China. We are on a ride at a fun park in Hong Kong, and the looks on our faces reflect our personalities and feelings regarding the ride, but more interesting is that our expressions are indicative of how we each felt about the move.

Sam looks calm and ready for the challenge ahead.

James is laughing and free of fear—mainly because he can't see what is in front of him.

Thomas looks scared and worried.

I look terrified!

As we laugh and consider our different personalities and responses to stress, Pearl invariably asks, "Where am I?"

We all pause to wonder. Where was our much-loved daughter and sister on March 31, 2008?

Was she homeless and living on the streets with a mother who was a drug addict? Was she somewhere in a village home watching her mother die? Was she lying alone in a room, vomiting and with diarrhoea?

We will never know where she was that day. But we do know that even then she was our daughter and God had planned for her to be part of our family.

Despite the photo on the fridge and the questions it raised, Pearl settled into life in Australia better than any of us. To her, it was filled with playgrounds, beaches, and doting friends and family. What else could a four-year-old want? She spoke fluently and happily to anyone willing to listen. She was loved by the doctors and nurses at the children's hospital when she had her checkups. She, in turn, thought the hospital was great. Every time she got a needle, they gave her a sticker! Not to mention that they took the blood from her arm rather than from the neck!

Occasionally I would try to speak to her in Chinese, at which point, she would loudly remind me that she is an Australian girl not a Chinese one.

She tried to copy everything I did, said, and wore. She became frustrated when she realized our clothes were different.

"Kids don't have to always look like their Mums," I tried to reassure her, telling her about her friends and how they dressed different from their mothers.

"But they all have Australian hair," she argued, "and I have Chinese hair. I want Australian hair like yours."

It was one of the only times that she mentioned that her differences worried her.

Pearl started school on February 1, 2012, exactly one year after we received her file in the mail, and less than four years after she was abandoned outside an Internet cafe in a city in central China. She was excited to try out her new school uniform complete with matching green hair bows. After a quick kiss, hug, and "I love you, Mum," she was gone, quickly camouflaged by all the other girls and boys in green. She proudly marched off to school, bearing a bulging backpack and plans of new friends and fun games and activities.

"Did you cry?" my friends ask.

"No, I didn't cry," I told them proudly. "I have run out of tears for her. I cried them all in China." I thought back to the many nights when Pearl cried herself to sleep when I wasn't beside her, and the nights I cried myself to sleep whilst awaiting her file.

I was proved wrong again just a few days later at Junior School Chapel. I had always loved attending chapel in the kid's Christian school, and both James and Pearl were excited to see me there. The children started off jumping and dancing to a few songs we didn't know, and despite having never heard the words, both Pearl and James joined in the excitement. The music then slowed to the final song, one we all knew well. 'Jesus loves me this I know, for the Bible tells me so.'

As the worship leader and children sang those famous words, Pearl craned to see me in the back row and gave me a thumbs up!

"This is our song," she seemed to be saying.

So there I stood, the mother who doesn't cry, with tears running down my face as I watched the little girl with matching green hair bows and remembered the dying orphan dressed in a garbage bag.

'Jesus loves me this I know, for the Bible tells me so. Little ones to Him belong, they are weak but He is strong.'

2012 and Beyond

Pearl leads a healthy happy life, much like any other five-year-old girl. She loves shopping, school, and ballet. She doesn't love bedtime, vegetables, or cleaning her room. Apart from taking medicine twice a day, she lives a normal life. The many people who comment on her bright, bubbly personality would never guess the life she had prior to 2008.

It is hard to believe that this little girl who was wanted by no one is now coming home with birthday party invitations. It is a miracle that she has gone from storage shed to school girl in four short years.

We have one of the first photos of her and Thomas in a frame on the TV. It sits next to the newborn photos of Thomas and James, just minutes after we met them.

One day when she was four years old, she picked it up and bought it to me. "Remember when I was at the orphanage and I was a boy? But then I turned into a girl."

I smiled at her belief that the shaved head had made her a boy, but I rejoice that she doesn't remember those four lonely months she spent 'as a boy' in an orphanage.

'Sing to the LORD! Give praise to the LORD!
He rescues the life of the needy from the hands of the wicked.'

—Jeremiah 20:13

Luke and Rose are now adopted and living in America. They are learning to speak English and are loved and cherished by their new family. They both bring so much joy to all who know them with their infectious giggles and dimples.

Their Mum wrote:

"Their arrival home and transition has been nothing short of incredible. While they miss China, their friends, and especially their Chinese mama, they have been really settling in at home. Luke loves to play with his blocks and he makes beautiful symmetrical buildings. He's also quite the cook! Rose loves her babies and is adept at making various beds and forts for them throughout the house. The other night we found three babies in our bed, all tucked in and ready for sleep! At bedtime, after they are all tucked in, we sound like the Walton family here. The kids start taking turns from across the hall. Our bedroom is about 10 feet from theirs. First We hear from Rose. "I love you, Mommy and I love you, Daddy!" and we say it back. Then Luke will chime in. "I love you. Daddy, I love you, Mommy!" and we say it back. This leads to the kids each taking a turn yelling, "Good night, Mommy! Good night, Daddy!" Then we say it back, which leads another round of "Sleep tight, Mommy" Sleep tight, Daddy!" It makes us laugh each time and is so sweet.

> *'In all their distress he too was distressed, and the angel of his presence saved them.*
>
> *In his love and mercy he redeemed them; he lifted them up and carried them all the days of old.'*
>
> —Isaiah 63:9

Little Lucy started school for the first time at nine years old. She proudly brings friends home to meet her Mum. They now live in a new apartment with heating and electricity. They are gradually learning how to become more independent and their self-esteem and confidence is improving.

Lucy had her first birthday party at nine years of age, which was attended by over fifty people! We were particularly encouraged to see the doctors from the infectious disease hospital there and also her cousins and uncle, who until recently had wanted no contact with her.

Things are still hard for them, and it is evident that they will always need help in caring for themselves, but every day they surprise us with the new skills they have learnt.

> Shout for joy, O heavens; rejoice, O earth; burst into song, O mountains!
>
> For the LORD comforts his people and will have compassion on his afflicted ones.
>
> —Isaiah 49:13

There are many books about adoption. Sam jokes that I have almost as many adoption books as I do self-help books. Every book tells a different story. A different child. A different set of circumstances and a different ending. But every book has similarities too.

God is the Father of the fatherless. He hears and answers the cry of the orphan. God is the God of the impossible. He can retrieve a file from America. He can bring families together against all odds.

Adoption truly is a miracle—the way it changes lives is beyond our wildest dreams.

I wrote Pearl's story in the hope that people will be encouraged to think of ways to help orphans in distress. Adoption, fostering, financial help, mission teams are only a few of the many ways to help.

In addition, I want people to stop telling us, "You are amazing." After reading this I want them to say, "Our God is amazing!"

I pray that, like Joseph, the harm that was meant for her can save the lives of many.

'Your ways, O God, are holy. What god is so great as our God?

You are the God who performs miracles; you display your power among the peoples.'

—Psalm 77:13–14